THE MAN IN SCARLET SOCKS

AN EXTRAORDINARY STORY OF AN ORDINARY MAN

PAUL HARRIS

Printed in the United Kingdom
First Printing, 2020

ISBN: 978-1-9163497-0-4 (Paperback)
ISBN: 978-1-9163497-1-1 (eBook)

Real Success Publishing
Solihull, West Midlands, B91 1UE

paul@real-success.co.uk

"God exists or does not exist. Leave it for us.
Your task is to learn how to live peacefully"

Dalai Lama

Foreword

Before you read David's story, you need to know just how ordinary he is.

Born in London, England, to Michael and Annie, he met Lucy Cartwright at the local youth club when they were just sixteen years old and were married at nineteen.

David joined his father's business, Turner Plumbing Supplies (TPS), after leaving school and he initially worked on the trade counter, before becoming a salesperson and eventually taking over the business from Michael.

Lucy worked in a local solicitors' firm in Muswell Hill and spent over twenty-five years at the same firm.

Their first child, Peter, was born after a year of marriage and was quickly followed by his sisters, Georgia and Annabel. The family live in a typical post-war semi-detached house near Waterlow Park in Hampstead Heath, London and they have stayed in this house all their married life.

Life continued for the family without any notably significant events until Peter, at eighteen years of age, purchased his first motorbike. This proved to be a fateful decision as, just a few months later, he was killed in a motorbike accident. This rocked the family to its core and life became extremely difficult. After a few years, they had slowly rebuilt their lives, but when TPS hit a difficult trading period David found himself struggling to keep the business afloat.

He slowly descended into a pit of despondency and found himself wondering if his life was worth living.

This wasn't a dramatic slide into depression, but a slow journey into despair.

This situation and David's life are not particularly extraordinary, and his story could be your story too.

Many families suffer financial hardship and difficulty. All families suffer loss, grief and ill health. So, if there is nothing particularly unusual about the place where David found himself, why do you need to read his story?

Well, this story is David's journey back from the depths of despair.

Ordinary lives can be transformed by extraordinary events. The unexpected can change your life, in the same way it has for David.

This is David's story.

PART
ONE

1.

D avid turned over in bed, uncomfortable and restless.

Lucy was facing away from him and in the moonlight filling the room, he noticed the contour of her body and watched it gently rise and fall with each breath. The silence of the room was suffocating, and his mind raced again with the idea he'd been considering for some time: Maybe his family could survive without him.

Lucy stirred as if picking up on his thoughts and turned over to face him. Her long, black hair fell across her face and he reached out to touch it, his fingers stopping just before her face. Somehow, she looked even more beautiful in her tangled state. Her breathing settled back into a regular rhythm and she fell back into a deep sleep. David, however, was wide awake, as he had been most mornings the previous few weeks. He'd tried every natural remedy he could find to help him sleep and eventually resorted to a trip to his doctor, who'd simply told him he was "stressed" and needed to learn to relax. He left the surgery with a prescription and a reassuring smile from the friendly doctor but no further forward in his attempts to ease the financial and emotional pressures he'd been facing.

David's thoughts were interrupted by a car driving past the house and the headlights filled the room. When they'd moved into their house on the corner, Lucy had said car headlights would disturb them at night. David had ignored her and convinced her all would be well. Convincing Lucy all would be well had become his daily pastime.

David thought about his father and wished he could speak to him about Turner Plumbing Supplies and how to save it. He recalled his father's pride when the doors first opened on his plumbing business and the smile on his face as he cut the ribbon on that first day. Then David remembered the day his father handed the business over to him and the broad smile as he shook David's hand. "It's in safe hands now," he'd said. But now, after ten years, the business was facing liquidation and David was facing bankruptcy. The past few years had seen a dramatic fall in demand in the construction industry and there was no sign of an upturn.

Lucy stirred again as if she could sense David's unease.

Another car swung around the bend into the estate and its lights lit up the bedroom once more. It was 5.30am and today's date was Peter's birthday, always a difficult one to get through these days. As the lights passed a picture on the wall, the faces of his three children jumped out as if a moment in time had been captured and released. It was a picture of Blackpool Tower and Annabel was on his shoulders with Georgia and Peter standing either side of him. It had been an amazing day and Lucy had kept the photograph, as it reminded her of when the children were small, and life was easy. But each time David looked at the photograph, his heart broke a little more.

The letter he'd received the previous day from the bank hadn't helped either. Lucy didn't know about that though.

As he watched her breathing peacefully in the bed next to him, David once more decided he didn't want to shatter her, particularly on what would have been Peter's birthday.

The day was challenging enough without having to tell the family they were about to lose their home too.

Having watched the car headlights sweep across the bedroom ceiling once more, David decided to get up. With thoughts about ending his own life still whirring around in his head, he felt he may as well try to make the most of another tough day in his life.

Gently pulling back the covers so as not to wake Lucy, he tiptoed across the bedroom floor, trying to avoid the squeaky floorboards which seemed to move their position on a regular basis. Whilst they'd improved their home over the years, he'd never managed to solve the problem of squeaky floorboards. They seemed to be a constant reminder of all that was wrong with his life. He grabbed the jogging gear and training shoes he'd neatly piled on the floor ready to pick up, and headed for the door.

As he crept downstairs, he could see some red roses and a red and white Arsenal scarf on the hall table, waiting to be taken to the cemetery. The sun was beginning to rise and as the gentle light created a glow in the room and he descended the stairs, he noticed a photograph next to the flowers. It was of Michael, his father, with Peter. They were standing in front of the motorbike Peter had purchased on his eighteenth birthday.

David reached the bottom of the stairs and began to pull on the jogging trousers, socks and sweater he wore for his morning walk. He balanced briefly on one leg as he did so, grabbing the table to steady himself. With this slight jolt, the photograph slipped from its position by the flowers and fluttered down, stopping at his feet. The streetlights beyond the front door seemed to glow over the photograph and David picked it up. He noticed some writing on the back. It said, *"To Peter, Remember – wherever you are and whatever you're doing, I'm always with you, love Grandpa".* David held the photograph in his hand and looked at the two people in his life he'd loved so dearly.

Michael had always been there for David to talk to. Living just a mile away in Hampstead Heath, David would often drop in on his way home and talk to his father about his plans, dreams and challenges. As David would leave, Michael would always say the same words – the same sentiment as he'd written to his grandson on the back of the photograph in David's hand. David placed the photograph in his jacket pocket.

As he stood up, he remembered he had a letter to post and he walked down the hall towards his home office. As he flicked on the light and the brightness startled his eyes, he saw the letter from the bank folded neatly on his desk. He opened the top drawer of the desk to hide it. As he pulled back the drawer, something caught his eye. He picked it up and held it in his hand. It was a medal from a collection Michael used to own and had given away items from to people at various points in their lives – usually when they were going through a difficult time. Those who received the medals were always grateful for Michael's thoughtfulness and David was proud of the way his father made others feel. On one side of the medal in his hand was a picture of an angel and on the other was a single word – 'Hope'.

The light above David's head flickered as if the bulb was about to blow. It went out for a moment and then flickered once more and then back on again. David looked up and concluded that there had been a power surge in the area.

He looked back at the medal in his hand and thought about his father. He smiled and placed the medal inside his jacket pocket, next to the photograph of his son and his father.

He turned off the light in the office and headed towards the front door. The house was still silent. Turning the latch, he picked up a set of keys from the hall table and stepped out into the gloomy light of a cool February morning. As he turned to pull the door closed, he noticed the roses and the Arsenal scarf. The scarf must have moved, as it was lying on the floor and although he began to think his imagination was running away with him, the scarf seemed to be folded into a heart shape. David dismissed his thoughts and pulled the door closed with a gentle click.

He pulled on his woolly hat and began to walk out of the cul-de-sac towards the main road and the park. He could hear the birds beginning their dawn chorus, but they were already drowned out by the hubbub of London traffic. People said New York was the city that never sleeps but David thought it applied to London too. He knew how they felt.

As he began to walk, he noticed that someone was walking slowly towards him. Even though the light was brightening and the streetlamps were still on, it was hard to make out if the person walking towards him was a man or a woman. As he approached the shuffling shape, he realised the person was carrying bags and using a walking stick for balance. It was clearly a vagrant who'd been sleeping in the park and was moving off before the crowds of early morning walkers would disturb or abuse them.

Just as he reached the bundle of bags and clothing, the shape raised its head.

"Good morning young man, it's a lovely day isn't it?"

It was an old lady, with a face so weather-worn it looked like her skin would crack and fall off her face at any moment. She was wearing a large, dirty coat at least two sizes too big and she had wellington boots on her feet which were different colours and both the same foot. Her hair was partially hidden under a neck scarf pulled over her head, but this didn't hide the knots and twisted curls of filthy hair peeking out. In one hand she carried two black bin bags full of her precious belongings and with the other she leant on an old walking stick.

As David reached her, she quickly raised her stick in front of his face. He thought she was going to hit him. He staggered backwards, nearly tripping over an uneven paving stone behind him.

"I said, it's a lovely day isn't it?" The lady was more insistent, and David decided it was best to agree with the old lady and let her pass. After all, she'd probably been drinking all night in the park and it wouldn't be the right time to challenge her.

"Er yes, I guess so," said David.

"Not good enough, young man. Every day is a good day when you're alive isn't it? Look over there!" She pointed towards the cemetery with her stick. "There are folk in that graveyard who'd love to be standing where you are this morning, so stop feeling sorry for yourself and celebrate this day."

Her accent puzzled David, as she clearly wasn't from London. In fact, she had no discernible accent at all.

"And it isn't just any day, young man – it's this day, the present day and it's your day!"

She lowered her stick and stepped towards him. As she did so, he caught the smell of sweat and decay. A wave of nausea hit him and for a moment he thought he was going to be sick. She stepped even closer towards him and looked at him directly.

"You see, David, Michael wouldn't want you to be thinking what you're thinking would he? You've got a family and some of us haven't. You carry on with your walk now and if you meet a few folks on the way, say hello to them for me, will you?" As she finished her sentence, she was already walking away from him.

David was frozen to the spot. How had she known his name or his father's name? He looked back towards the old lady, who was moving slowly away from him and called out to her.

"How do you know my name?"

Without turning back towards him, she called out, "It's my job to know your name."

David's feet were rooted to the spot. He wanted to go and speak to the old lady again to find out what she knew about him.

The air was clear and cold. David's breath was visible in the large plumes of vapour circling around him. He turned back to look at the park and the cemetery beyond, wondering if he should go home or press on with his walk. He turned to ask the old lady one more question, but she was gone.

David felt his feet move and his legs began to take him onwards towards the park. His mind was racing from his encounter with the old bag-lady. She'd said every day was a lovely day, but it didn't make sense to him. How could someone with so few possessions and with very little hope in her life see the new day as a lovely day?

As he continued to walk towards the park, he heard the rattle of milk bottles as a milk float turned the corner ahead of him. It began to move along the road towards where David was walking. As the milk float whirred its way towards him and the bottles clinked, David could hear the milkman whistling. He recognised the tune. It was 'Oh, What a Beautiful Morning' from the stage show Oklahoma. As the milk float began to pass, the milkman called out to him above the whirr of the electric engine and the rattle of the bottles. "It's a lovely day isn't it?"

"If you say so!" called David.

The milk float passed by and the whistling from the milkman continued until the milk float turned a corner beyond where David was standing. He was once again rooted to the spot. It was most definitely not a lovely day and he wondered why the first two people he'd met had both said the same thing to him.

David turned to walk into Highgate Park and as he approached the cast iron gate at the entrance, he could hear a bird chirping loudly off to his right-hand side. He looked up towards the bird which was sat on top of the railings. It was a plump, red robin and as he walked towards the bird, it cocked its head to one side as if curious about David's presence. It chirped again loudly, moving its head from side to side as if he couldn't quite work out why David was there or why he looked glum.

"Do you think it's a lovely day then mate?" asked David.

The robin just chirped and tweeted back at David, clearly happy to be alive and in the park.

David stepped forward and the robin jumped off the railing onto the gate. As he opened the gate and stepped into the park, the robin didn't move. It just allowed David to open the gate and close it gently again, with the robin still perched and chirping away merrily.

"Have a lovely day," said David towards the robin and he entered the park.

Waterlow Park (known as Highgate Park to locals) is a beautiful and peaceful place in the heart of north London. It has its origins in the Victorian era when affluent, rich and often famous people began to settle in the area. With three large ponds providing a water supply to the local homes, it became an important part of Victorian life, with several prominent families building homes in the park.

David walked towards the Middle Pond in the park. Despite its location in the heart of London, the park felt like a sanctuary and David found it lifted his spirits. He'd lived near the park for most of his life and yet only recently had he truly understood its value to him.

The park was quiet, and as the sun continued to rise, an eerie mist rose up from the ground as the moisture on the grass was warmed and began to evaporate. It was as if the ground beneath his feet was gently burning with the smoke of a new day. David increased the speed of his walk to increase his heart rate, just as his doctor had suggested.

He followed the path beyond the Middle Pond and as he headed across the park, he could see a figure sitting on a park bench ahead of him. It was still cold and early in the morning, so he wondered if it was another vagrant who had spent the night outdoors, drunk on alcohol and relying on the generosity of passers-by for food and warmth. But as David got closer to the figure on the bench, he could see it was a well-dressed man in a dark suit wearing a matching trilby hat. The man didn't have a warm coat and as David got within a few metres, he could see the man's breath emerging from his nostrils.

David intended to walk straight past and avoid eye contact so he could finish his walk, but as he got close, the man looked up and their eyes met.

"Good morning. It's a lovely day isn't it?" he said.

Without slowing his stride, David continued to walk past. "I suppose so," he said, puzzled why everyone he'd met so far had said the same thing to him.

"But you don't really think that do you David?" the man replied.

David stopped abruptly, and his feet slipped on the dew-covered pavement. He swung around quickly and faced the man.

"How do you know my name?"

"That's not important, my friend. But what is important now is for you to stop a while and chat to an old man who simply wants to help you."

David didn't know whether to run or sit down. His breath quickened, blowing clouds of vapour in the air. The man simply smiled back at him with a warmth that filled the cold air alongside the sunshine beginning to emerge above the London skyline.

"Please, young man, just take a few moments to sit with me. I think you'll find it time well spent."

David's feet moved almost involuntarily and in an instant he was seated on the left of the man on the cold park bench.

"Thank you," said the man.

David was confused, but strangely, felt no fear. He glanced at the man and it was clear he was not a vagrant as he'd first thought. He was dressed in a dark blue pinstripe suit with a waistcoat and a white shirt with an old-fashioned pin-collar with studs on both sides. He wore a dark blue tie matching his suit. In his breast pocket, a crisp white handkerchief poked out. The man turned towards David and lifted his hat with his right hand.

"Good to meet you David."

David could feel the coldness of the bench and the air around him continued to be filled with the vapour of their breath. He looked at the man and could see he was older, maybe in his seventies. His face was round and around his pale blue eyes were wrinkles. He wore circular, silver rimmed spectacles which sat perfectly straight across his nose. His dark blue trilby hat revealed just the edges of his pure, neatly trimmed white hair. Everything about the man was smart, neat and in its place.

Then David's eyes were drawn to something that really didn't fit with this perfectly tailored image. Between his smart black brogue shoes and the sharply creased trouser legs of his suit, was a flash of scarlet, the colour of his socks. David somehow hadn't noticed them as he'd walked towards him but now, sitting next to him, he couldn't take his eyes off them. David thought the man had chosen the worst possible pair of socks to match his suit. They looked completely out of place and ruined his neat and smart appearance.

"But sometimes, not everything is perfect, is it David?"

David looked up, embarrassed he'd been spotted staring at the man's scarlet socks and continuing to be intrigued as to how the old man knew his name.

"Who are you?" asked David.

"I'm Michael. I've just told you. I see lots of people walk through this park during the day, from the early risers like you to the late-night strollers who've maybe had a little too much to drink. It saddens me to see you struggling to deal with your lives. Just like you David, many others think life has become too hard. It's such a shame."

"You mean you sit in this park all day talking to people? That's crazy!"

"No. I simply hear their thoughts David. And then I try to help in the best way I can."

David wondered if the man was confused and lost.

"Do you live in a home nearby? Can I call someone for you?"

"No, I'm fine thank you. Don't worry about me David. I live in all sorts of places."

David quickly decided it was time to leave the strange old man on the bench and get on with his walk. He began to get up and leave when Michael grabbed his arm.

"Sit down please David. You've nothing to fear and I'm here to help you."

David slumped back onto the bench. "But how do you know who I am? This is crazy. You're crazy. I just want to go home."

"I know it's all a little unsettling David, but you must trust me. After all, I know that you're considering taking your own life and that's a big step to take isn't it?"

Michael said this in such a matter-of-fact way that for a moment David didn't register what had been said. But then it hit him, and he looked again at this man with the scarlet socks and wondered how he could possibly know his darkest thoughts. And yet, perversely, instead of sending a chill down his spine, David found that an entirely different feeling stirred within him. It was a warm feeling deep inside his soul, filling his body. He grappled with his sense of wanting to run with his desire to stay and listen to this old man. He recognised the feeling and he remembered the medal he'd placed in his pocket. The feeling emerging within him was... 'Hope'...

"It saddens me David, just how many people think the cemetery is a better place for them than the park."

David shuffled uncomfortably as the traffic in the distance continued to produce its low hum. He felt the silence and shivered – not with the cold, but with something else he couldn't work out. It felt like an anticipation of something – as if the man had some important news for him. David could hear a police car siren somewhere outside the park and he wondered who was in difficulty and needed help.

"I have no idea why I'm here, or who you are. Why do you want to speak to me?"

Michael turned towards him and smiled. "I'm simply here to help but you must be ready to accept it."

"I'm not good at accepting help and anyway, how do you know you can help me?"

"Because it's my job David. I'm going to show you how to rebuild your life."

"What? How can you do that? I don't understand what this is all about or why I'm sitting here with you. This is crazy."

Michael looked directly at him. "I understand David, but it's been organised, and you're meant to be here with me, so let's not waste time. Let's get started. Tell me, have you ever set goals or had dreams for yourself in life?"

"Hang on. What do you mean it's been organised? Did Lucy set this up?"

"No David. The Governor organises everything. All you need to do is stop wasting time and answer my question."

"Who's the Governor? Are you working for someone?"

The old man looked directly at David and lowered his voice. "We all work for someone, don't we? Let's stop wasting time and get on. You haven't achieved your goals and dreams yet and you never did get the house with the gravel drive, did you?"

David spun round towards Michael. "How on earth do you know about my dream to own a house with a gravel drive? In fact, how can you know anything about me? We haven't met before!"

"I know everything about you David. It's why I'm here and why I'm going to show you there is a different way for you to live. The world works in a different way to how you've always understood it. I'm going to show you that the world you live in is, in fact, upside down, back to front and the wrong way around. It's a truly beautiful paradox." He chuckled to himself.

"That's crazy! The world is just what it is, and I've never met you before. And what do you mean, it's upside down and back to front? This is insane. In fact, you're insane. I need to go now."

David started to rise again from the bench, but Michael was unfazed.

"Maybe you're looking in the wrong place for your hopes and dreams," said Michael. "Have you ever considered that?" He held David's gaze, looking at him over his glasses.

David hadn't considered anything other than mere survival for several years. The business his father had taken years to build up was in danger of insolvency due to a market-driven collapse of the construction market caused by the biggest recession since the second world war. His dreams had faded, and his hopes had become nothing more than being able to put food on the table.

"Dreams just disappoint you," said David.

"OK David, this is a big problem with many people in your world; you think you know what you want from your life and seek more and more things to fill it. You build pictures and dreams around having things you believe will bring happiness further down the line. When you achieve your dreams, you feel no different because often, they're built around what you think you should have, based on comparison with others rather than what your heart really desires."

David knew he'd often looked around at others and compared himself to them. "But there's nothing wrong with wanting more is there?"

"No, not at all," he replied. "But wanting more and dreaming big isn't always the answer. You aim for big things because your teachers and leaders say you should aim high and demand more from your lives. Your society is based around having bigger and better 'things' and getting them as fast as you can. You're constantly told you shouldn't settle with what you have but must constantly strive for more. But what happens to those who are happy with achieving something smaller? What happens if they aim too high? What happens to their happiness then?"

David thought about some of his friends who lived what he perceived to be a more holistic or spiritual lifestyle and were always talking about being happy with what they'd got. This view seemed prevalent among his religious friends too and religion was something he'd turned away from a long time ago. He thought they were unambitious, slow and destined to live a life of mediocrity and boredom.

"But the problem in aiming lower is that you end up with less; surely that makes you unhappy?"

"Who told you having less makes you unhappy?" said Michael.

"You're twisting my words now. I didn't say having less makes you unhappy. I said accepting less than you could have can make you unhappy."

"Yes, David but let me ask you again. Who told you accepting less makes you unhappy?"

"Morning Michael!"

It was another voice from behind David, who turned to see a man jogging towards them. He wore headphones which looked like earmuffs. He was wearing a light blue shell suit from an era long past and his running shoes were dirty and scuffed.

"Morning Sid," said Michael. "It's a lovely day isn't it?"

"Sure is, Michael. And how are you doing?" He'd stopped in front of David but didn't acknowledge his presence. He also continued to jog on the spot, not wishing to tighten up and get cold.

"I'm good thank you Sid."

"Well, can't stop, got to get home to Margaret. She'll be wondering where I've got to!"

"I know, Sid. You take care."

The man turned and continued off towards the edge of the park. David was puzzled as to why the man didn't say hello to him.

He suddenly felt very cold, the freshness of the morning air once again biting at his clothes.

"How did you know Sid?" David asked.

"I've already told you David. It's my job to know people. Listen, it's time you got back home too or else your family will also be wondering where you are. I think we've talked enough for today."

Michael rose from the bench and put out his hand. David took it and felt a warmth from the old man that felt like electricity rising up his arm.

"I will see you again David."

"I hope so Michael. Thanks for talking to me this morning."

Michael turned and walked off towards the cemetery at the edge of the park. David stood motionless, watching the old man with scarlet socks walk away, wondering what had just happened. As if sensing David was watching him, Michael lifted his hat to acknowledge him.

David looked around the park to see if anyone had been present to watch his encounter with Michael. On a cast iron waste basket a few yards away sat the robin that had greeted him at the entrance to the park. He was chirping away merrily and constantly moving his head to survey the area around him.

David laughed to himself. He felt brighter somehow, and it was as if the little robin knew it. It flew off towards a nearby oak tree and David decided he needed to head home, as Lucy would be getting up and wondering why he wasn't back from his walk. But how could he tell her about what had happened and his encounter with Michael? Maybe it would be best to just keep it to himself for now.

David turned and realised his legs felt stiff as if he'd been sitting for some time. He thought about the jogger called Sid who had been wearing clothes from a different era.

A memory stirred. David remembered a Sid Sims who worked for his Dad in the yard in the 1980s and how he'd loved to run. And he wore shell suits when he ran.

David stood still. As he looked down at the bench where he'd been sitting with Michael, attached to the slats forming the back of the bench was a brass plaque with some words engraved, which David read slowly.

'This bench is provided to the people of Highgate in memory of Sid and Margaret Sims who used to sit here and hold hands.'

David realised the runner in the shell suit he'd just met was Sid Sims. And Sid was dead.

2.

David left the park and headed home in a daze, light-headed and wondering if he was in some sort of dream. But he felt lighter and somehow invigorated. His meeting with Michael made little sense and yet, strangely, it felt good. It was a paradox of emotions and whilst it should have made him question his sanity, he felt clearer in his thoughts than he had for some time.

He thought about Michael and his smart suit and bright red socks and wondered if he'd see him again. And he thought about Sid Sims, the man who years ago had sat on the bench with his wife Margaret but who somehow had now visited them all in the park.

David had always believed that there was something beyond death. As his father had been a Roman Catholic and his mother a Methodist, heaven and hell were lively topics in his childhood. They had been the subject of many rows and arguments around the meal table, particularly on a Sunday when his parents had come back from their respective churches. However, after Peter died, David had turned away from Christianity and any form of mainstream religion. When David had watched Peter set off for a ride on his new motorbike, David had never expected that the next time he would see him would be in hospital to say goodbye. From that moment, David was convinced that no God could exist that would allow such a terrible burden to be cast upon their family.

As he arrived back at his front door, he felt inside his pocket for his keys and touched the medal. He pulled out his keys and the medal was with them, falling onto the floor. He reached down and picked it up. The word on the medal was 'Faith'. David was certain that he'd left the house with a medal which had 'Hope' engraved on it. And yet now, somehow, he'd returned with a medal that had the word 'Faith' on it instead.

He stood on the doorstep holding his keys in one hand and the medal in the other.

"It's a lovely day isn't it?" It was the same milkman he'd seen earlier, now placing two milk bottles outside the house next door. He picked up two empty bottles and looked at David.

"It's funny how life can seem empty at times but can be filled up really quickly, ain't it?"

He winked at David and headed back to his milk float, whistling merrily. The cheery milkman was soon back on his float and drove around the corner out of sight.

David took a deep breath and turned to unlock his front door. Just as he did so, the door opened and Lucy was stood in front of him in her dressing gown, her hair untidy around her shoulders and looking like she'd just got out of bed.

"Why are you standing here?" she said.

"I was just chatting to the milkman next door," David replied.

Lucy leaned forward and peered next door. "Milkman? There hasn't been a milkman on this road since Jerry came around ten years ago. Maybe they've finally replaced him. Seems a bit strange though after all these years. Did he call at many other houses, as you could've asked him to call here?"

David wondered about the milkman. The milk float did look a bit old; maybe ten years out of date. He turned and looked at the front step of his next-door neighbour and there were no milk bottles on the step. Stepping back into the house, David changed the subject.

"I had a lovely walk this morning. I met some interesting people too!"

Lucy was walking down the hall towards the kitchen. "Must be as crazy as you then to be out so early in the morning."

David headed for the stairs and up to the bathroom where he got out of his clothes and showered. The events of the last hour or so began to replay in his mind. He wondered if it was all just a daydream. Perhaps Michael had just been a figment of his imagination and perhaps Sid was not some ghost from the past but was indeed just a runner with bad taste in tracksuits. But it had all felt very real and Michael had said he'd meet him again.

As David dried himself, the reality of the day ahead began to dawn on him, and familiar thoughts returned. He entered his bedroom and opened a drawer in his wardrobe and pulled out some underwear. As he pulled on his boxer shorts and socks, he remembered the bright red socks Michael wore and how out of place they seemed with the rest of his attire. But Michael had said his socks were still part of who he was, even though they seemed out of place.

David wondered which parts of his life were out of place. He knew his business was struggling and money had been tight for the past couple of years. He also knew that losing his son at such an early age had blown a hole in his life that could never be filled. But as he thought of Annabel, Georgia and Lucy, he realised how much of his life was full of love. He thought about what the strange milkman had said to him. Perhaps his life was fuller than he previously thought.

As he got dressed into his work clothes, the heaviness of responsibility weighed on his mind. The bank was chasing him for repayments on his business premises and he was also behind on the mortgage. The recession had hit hard, and business had been difficult. Plumbing was meant to be one of the professions least affected by any sudden downturn in the economy, but it didn't feel like that at TPS. Business had been poor for some time, with little sign of any imminent improvement.

"It'll pass," his father had said, as he tried to reassure him. He'd said that all recessions are cyclical and eventually the market would recover. David yearned to be able to speak to his father again, as he had always been an eternal optimist. Nothing seemed to faze him. Even when Peter died, his father had quickly turned to his faith for comfort, spending many hours with a priest, praying and finding peace. Peace was something David yearned for but had now eluded him for so long that he had forgotten what it felt like. He thought perhaps you had to be dead to truly find peace.

He headed downstairs and the smell of freshly cooked toast filled the air. The girls were both sitting at the breakfast table in the kitchen looking at their phones and Lucy was busying herself preparing breakfast for them. It irritated David that Lucy insisted on making their breakfast for them when they were both clearly capable of making it for themselves. It annoyed him even more that they just sat looking at their phones, no doubt on social media chatting to their friends, whilst their mother prepared their breakfast.

"Morning, Dad," said Annabel. Georgia just grunted something which David couldn't make out.

"Morning to you too. Haven't you got anything better to do than look at your phones all the time?"

"Don't be grumpy Dad," said Annabel, who was always cheery in the morning, unlike her sister, who barely said a word before she left the house each day.

"Would you like some scrambled egg?" asked Lucy, looking at David.

"Yes please. I need to be out pretty quickly though."

"Well, it's ready now. Sit down and I'll serve it up."

Everything seemed so 'normal'. David sat in the chair opposite his two daughters and observed how their worlds hadn't changed from the previous day. Even though it was Peter's birthday, which each year was a difficult day, everything else appeared to be the same. But David felt different. He felt he was in a different house from the day before. He couldn't place the feeling but there was a lightness which hadn't been there before.

"Are you heading up to see Peter today girls?" asked David.

"We always go up to see him on his birthday – you know that," said Lucy, slightly annoyed that David would think they weren't thinking about Peter on his birthday.

"I'll go up after work Dad," said Georgia.

"Me too," said Annabel and she returned to her mobile phone along with her sister.

David began to think about the day ahead. There were some big contracts coming up and his team of plumbers would be in the depot to collect their supplies. It was going to be a busy day.

"What are you smiling at?" asked Lucy as she placed a plate of scrambled egg on toast in front of him. "You look like the cat that got the cream."

"I wasn't aware I was smiling," said David.

"Perhaps it's chatting to those folks you met in the park this morning?" suggested Lucy as she returned to the sink and began washing up the pan she'd used to make breakfast.

"Maybe," said David.

As he tucked into his scrambled egg and toast and his daughters ate their own breakfasts while still typing into their phones, David recognised the feeling inside. It was only tiny and barely recognisable, but it was real. He'd felt it earlier. It was hope. And he wondered if today was indeed going be a lovely day.

3.

David's day had been pretty much as he'd expected. The bank had called, wanting to discuss his business mortgage, with another department calling to chase him for the arrears on his personal mortgage. Both calls did nothing to reduce the pressures on his finances or help his wellbeing.

Although the challenges remained, after a more buoyant day's trading, David returned home feeling a little better about the present and the future. He wondered if things were showing some glimmers of beginning to get better. As he put the key in the door to step into the house, he recognised the feeling he was coming home with. He put his hand in his pocket and pulled out the angel medal. The word on the medal was 'Faith,' just as it had been that morning, when he'd returned home from his walk. Over breakfast he'd felt a feeling of hope and as he returned home, he sensed the feeling of faith.

He stopped, pulling the key back out of the door. The fact that today would have been Peter's 25th birthday was of course the biggest shadow falling across the day. Far more so than any money or business issues. It had been on his mind all day, so he wanted to visit his son's grave before he went back into the house. He remembered there was a small chapel near the crematorium, and he decided he wanted to go there to say a prayer, which was something he hadn't done for a long time. He pulled the front door shut and headed towards the park and the cemetery beyond.

The day had remained sunny and bright and although the light was fading, the sky was a bright red.

As he walked towards the park, he thought about Michael. Not his father, but the old man with the red socks. As he arrived at the gate, the robin which had cheerfully greeted him earlier was nowhere to be seen. David opened the gate and headed into the park, walking past the bench where he'd sat and onwards to the cemetery and crematorium.

As he reached Peter's remembrance stone, he could see that Lucy, Annabel and Georgia had already been to visit. There were birthday cards from the girls and roses had been placed in a vase in front of the stone. As Peter had been cremated, there wasn't much space between each headstone, so flowers and cards often fell from neighbouring stones onto the area next to them. One of the roses from Peter's grave had blown onto the next stone and so he picked it up to move it back.

"My wife loved roses," said a voice from behind him.

David swung round. A tall man stood behind him wearing a long, black coat, black cap, black gloves and black shoes. There was an eeriness to him and as David stood up, he realised how tall the man was too. He was staring at the headstone next to Peter's.

"I'm sorry," said David. "I was just moving the rose back but please have it for your wife" and he proffered the rose towards the man.

The man didn't move. "No thank you. I've not touched a rose since she passed. As she loved them, I can't bear to look at them, as it reminds me of what I've lost."

David wasn't sure how to comfort the man or indeed where he'd come from, as he hadn't heard him walk along the path.

"When did you lose her?" asked David.

"Time makes no difference to the pain does it? It's endless and it never goes away."

The man looked incredibly sad. His face was etched with lines and his grey hair peeking beneath his hat was unkempt and uncared for. David guessed he was in his sixties and wondered if he had any hope or was just rooted in despair.

"I'm going to the chapel to say a prayer for my son," said David. "Would you like to come with me?"

The man looked at David with such sorrowful eyes that David's heart wept for the man. He had never encountered such deep sadness and similar emotions began to well up inside him.

David said, "I haven't been inside a church or a chapel since my son died but something happened to me today to give me hope and faith, so I've decided to say thank you in the chapel. Come with me and maybe you'll find some peace?"

The man looked at David again and then held out his hand. "Samuel Hutchinson. Pleased to meet you."

David took Samuel's gloved hand and shook it warmly. "David Turner and it's good to meet you Samuel."

The two men walked away from the sadness of the headstones of their beloved relatives and headed towards the chapel.

"How did you lose your wife and what was her name? I'm sorry, I've never noticed the names on the stones around Peter."

"It's OK. I know what it's like to stand and stare at a single stone. Her name was Lucia and she was Italian. A real firebrand too. Full of life and energy. We were together for thirty years before she passed."

"I'm so sorry Samuel. How did you lose her?"

"Cancer. Started in her breast and moved quickly around her body. The woman who left me looked nothing like the woman I'd married and loved for all those years."

"That must've been awful to see and to watch her suffer."

"But you lost your son in an accident when his life was just beginning. That is far worse!"

"How do you know my son died in an accident?" David asked, surprised Samuel would know the facts around Peter's death.

"The inscription on the headstone," said Samuel. "I've often stood and wondered how your family coped with losing your son Peter at such a young age. There are some heart-breaking stories if you take the time to read the cards, messages and inscriptions on the headstones in this cemetery."

David felt a wave of guilt pass over him. He'd never taken the time to read the headstones either side of Peter's, let alone in the rest of this huge cemetery. And yet, Samuel knew about his son.

"How often do you come to the cemetery Samuel?"

"Every day for the past 10 years. Never miss a day. I've not been away from home since she died, as there doesn't seem any point. This gives me some comfort and rhythm to my life, even if some would consider this to be a depressing place to spend time. But I find it peaceful."

They arrived at the crematorium and walked around the right-hand side to the door of the chapel.

"Shall we go in?" asked David.

Samuel grabbed the handle of the door and opened the door, inviting David to enter first.

They stepped through the door and Samuel pulled it too behind them. As the door clicked shut, the hum of London traffic disappeared and all that remained was a dull silence.

"Where shall we sit?" whispered David, respecting the silence surrounding them.

"Over there," said Samuel, pointing to a few chairs on the right-hand side of the chapel.

Candles were burning on a small altar at the back of the chapel and the smell of candle wax filled the air. There was a single, plain wooden cross on the top of the altar, framed by a large stained-glass window behind. The evening sun was shining through the colourful image of Jesus Christ being crucified on the cross. Above the image of Jesus were the words, 'O death where is your victory, O death where is your sting?' engraved into the glass.

"Corinthians 1, chapter 5, verse 55," said Samuel.

"Gosh, how do you know?" asked David.

"I used to be a minister, but I lost my faith when my Lucia died. I was angry with God and turned away from him. I gave up my ministry and lost all hope. This is the first time I've been back in a church since she died."

"Let's sit down, Samuel," and David gestured to a few chairs.

Samuel sat down and removed his cap, placing it on the chair next to him. He smoothed down his unkempt hair as if feeling he should tidy himself up. He sat looking up at the image of Jesus in the stained-glass window and cocked his head to one side. "Can you see?"

David looked up towards the window.

"Look there," said Samuel. "Above his head. Look at his halo."

David looked at the image of Jesus and above his head, his halo glowed. The evening sun was highlighting his halo and it stood out in the image.

David turned back towards Samuel who was smiling.

"That's nice," he said.

David hadn't prayed for a long time but on such a significant date, he wanted to say something to show how much he still loved Peter. All he could remember was The Lord's Prayer.

"Shall we say The Lord's Prayer Samuel?"

"Yes, that would be nice."

Then, in the silence of the empty chapel, with the noise of London shut out behind the closed door and the evening sun streaming through the stained-glass window, David and Samuel spoke The Lord's Prayer together. It was a moment of empathy and connection David had not felt for some time. Once they'd finished the prayer they sat for a while before Samuel broke the silence.

"Empathy is often the only cure for despair."

"Sorry, what do you mean Samuel?"

Samuel was staring ahead at the stained-glass window.

"Despair is like a deep, dark well David and I know it's a place you've visited. It's the place many of us encounter when life goes badly, when we lose someone we love or simply can't cope with what life throws at us. We find ourselves at the bottom of the deep, dark well of despair where there is no light and no way out."

"I do know that place," said David. "I was there when we lost Peter and I've been there often recently. Life just seems too tough to endure at times doesn't it?"

"Yes David, but there is a way out."

Samuel turned to look at David. "You see David, when I lost Lucia, I spiralled into a well of depression, despair and alcohol-fuelled oblivion. Nothing I did or thought would take away the pain. Doctors prescribed pills and counsellors offered advice, but I couldn't connect with anything they said."

David recalled the days after Peter's death and how he was prescribed sleeping pills. He only took them for a few days before stopping, as they simply numbed him into a zombie-like existence. He knew it wasn't the answer.

"My friends and family tried to help too," Samuel added. "They'd invite me round to their houses for dinner where I'd sit with other couples and hear them talking about their plans. They tried to be sympathetic, but they could never understand how I felt. I stopped seeing them and I shut myself off from the world."

David knew Samuel's pain. He understood the desire to shut out the world and to turn away from those who you love.

David placed his hand on Samuel's shoulder, a man he had only met for a few moments, but whom he felt he'd known all his life.

"I hear you Samuel. I know what it's like to lose someone you love and how crippling and suffocating it can be. Many will be sympathetic, and some will even offer solutions and advice, but I can see that I have empathy Samuel. I truly do."

"Yes David, I know you do. I understand your despair and you understand mine. In this connection we will both heal in a way no other form of healing can provide."

Samuel took David's hand and placed his own gloved hand on top of his. "Today you said you began with hope and ended with faith, and in sharing this time with me, you've given me hope and restored a little of my faith. Being here with you and seeing the light of Jesus once more, I think I can begin to move forwards. Thank you."

David was shocked and touched by Samuel's words. Just by being present with this man who he'd never met before and taking some time to sit in silence with him, his faith in life had been energised. It was a powerful moment that lifted David.

Samuel was weeping gently next to David, who turned back to face the altar and the stained-glass window. He held Samuel's hand as he gently sobbed tears of relief.

Samuel reached into his coat pocket and pulled out a handkerchief to wipe away his tears. Samuel wiped his eyes and returned the handkerchief to his pocket.

"Thank you, David," said Samuel. "I'll leave you now and hope to see you again in the cemetery. It's been a pleasure to meet you."

Samuel turned and walked out of the chapel, shutting the door behind him.

After a few moments, David turned and left the chapel, walking briskly through the park towards his home. The light had nearly faded completely from this strange but uplifting day. David arrived back at the house and put the key in the door, this time entering and looking forward to seeing his family.

4.

"How was your day?" said Lucy as David walked into the kitchen.

"Good thanks. Trade was pretty brisk – or at least it felt that way anyway."

David sat down at the kitchen table as Lucy was busy preparing some food at the cooker where sizzling sounds and spicy smells were being generated. "Smells good, what's for supper?"

"Chicken tikka masala – your favourite," replied Lucy. She turned to face David for the first time since he'd entered the room. David noticed her make-up was smudged around her eyes as if she'd been crying.

"Are you OK love?" asked David.

"Yeah, of course I am. Blooming onions made me cry that's all."

David wasn't convinced. "I went to see Peter and met a lovely man while I was there. His wife has a remembrance stone next to Peter's."

Lucy had turned back to continue with preparing the curry and the smells continued to rise from the pan in front of her. "What's his name?" she said.

"Samuel Hutchinson. He used to be a minister but lost his faith when his wife died. We went into the chapel and said The Lord's Prayer together. It was nice and I felt sort of peaceful."

Lucy turned around quickly. "Crikey, you went into the chapel, did you? I've tried to get you back into church lots of times, but you've always refused."

"I know Lucy, but having been to Peter's grave, I just wanted to find some peace and the chapel seemed as good a place as any to try to find it. It lifted me and gave me hope for the future."

Lucy looked very surprised. "Gosh, maybe there is hope for us all if you can feel that way. It's strange though, as I met a lovely lady when I was putting the roses on Peter's grave." Lucy turned down the gas underneath the pan she'd been working on and sat down at the kitchen table opposite David.

"I'd been tidying up the area around Peter's stone and I was a little lost in my thoughts when a lady came up behind me and asked me if she could have one of my roses. She said she loved roses."

David shivered. "What was her name?"

"I couldn't remember at first, but she was tall and looked Italian or Spanish or something like that. She was a very pretty lady, dressed smartly in a blue coat and scarf. She had lovely eyes too and when she looked at me, I felt... well, I'm not sure how to describe it really... like something good was happening. A bit like you really, and that maybe there was hope for us. It was very strange."

David's mind was whirring. "What did she do with the rose?"

"Well, that's the strange thing. She just leant down and put it on the stone next to Peter's. Then she thanked me and walked away towards the crematorium."

"Are you sure you can't remember her name?" asked David, shaking with anticipation.

David felt lightheaded. He had a feeling that the lady was Lucia, Samuel's late wife, but it didn't make sense.

"She was a lovely lady though, so I was happy to leave the rose on the stone whoever she was. Quite a coincidence though David?"

"Er yes... I suppose so," spluttered David.

"Are you OK David? You've gone very pale."

"Yes, I'm fine, it's just been quite a long day." David got up from the table. "I'm going to jump in the shower and freshen up before we eat, is that OK?"

"Sure," said Lucy. "I'll crack on with getting supper ready. The girls are in their rooms so let them know food will be ready in about ten minutes."

David walked out of the kitchen and climbed the stairs. He could hear the televisions going in both the girls' bedrooms so he shouted to them that supper would be ready in ten minutes. They both acknowledged him, and he headed for the bedroom. As he began to undress, he noticed the perspiration on his body. He'd been sweating but he felt cold, as if he was coming down with something. He headed for the bathroom and turned on the shower. Removing his boxer shorts, he got into the shower and felt the warm water flow over his body.

His mind raced with thoughts about the lady who Lucy had met in the cemetery. It must have been Samuel's wife Lucia. It had to be. But that would mean she was some sort of ghost, just like Sid Sims. But David didn't believe in ghosts, apparitions or spirits. He believed there was no such thing.

"Supper's ready!" called Lucy from downstairs. Almost in harmony and certainly in complete synchronisation, David, Annabel and Georgia all shouted, "OK."

David pulled on some tracksuit bottoms and a t-shirt and headed downstairs. As he left the bedroom, he met Annabel at the top of the stairs. "How was your day?" he asked.

"Great thanks – I was helping out in class today and the kids were fab." Annabel worked as a teaching assistant at the St Joseph's Catholic primary school, just the other side of Highgate cemetery. "Mrs Jones was pleased with the work I did with Imran today too, as he seemed a little calmer."

They got to the bottom of the stairs and headed for the kitchen.

"Smells great Mum, how was your day?"

David sat back down at the kitchen table and smiled inwardly at Annabel's optimism. She was always bright and bubbly, as if nothing seemed to faze her. It reminded David of his own father and how he'd always maintained a positive attitude towards life – whatever it threw at him.

"My day was OK thanks Annabel. I went across to see Peter and I saw your card. That was thoughtful."

"Yes, I put it there on my way to school this morning. In fact, I had quite a strange thing happen to me in the park as I walked through."

"Oh yes?" said Lucy who continued to serve up the supper onto four plates.

"Yes, as I was walking through the park, there was an old man sitting on one of the benches as you head towards the cemetery. As I walked towards him, I could see he was smiling. Next to him on the bench was a beautiful robin which was chirping and calling away. It was almost like they were having a conversation."

"What did the old man look like?" said David, his curiosity piqued.

"Oh, I can't remember really but he wore a dark suit and a dark blue hat a bit like Grandad used to wear. What was odd though was that he had bright red socks on. I could see them clearly as I walked up to him."

David smiled. "I think I met him too on my morning walk."

Lucy put plates of chicken tikka masala and rice down in everyone's place. "Sounds like you both saw the same chap then." Lucy then went out of the kitchen to call again for Georgia who hadn't appeared.

"I'm coming," shouted Georgia from upstairs.

"Did the man say anything to you Annabel?" asked David.

"No Dad, he seemed more intent on having his conversation with the robin sat next to him on the bench. But he did smile at me as I went past. He seemed very pleased with himself. I just thought he was a cheery old man and it made me feel good."

Georgia appeared in the kitchen. She'd clearly fallen asleep on her bed as her hair was unkempt and she wore no make-up. She shuffled around to her seat at the table and sat down. She picked up a fork and started eating. The difference in the personalities between Annabel and Georgia was as starkly different as their physical appearances. Georgia was blond, short and slightly curvier than her younger sister, who was tall, slim and dark. Both had elements of David and Lucy's personalities, but Annabel certainly carried Lucy's optimistic and bubbly outlook on life, whereas Georgia was more like David. If there was a glass to be observed by Georgia and David, it was generally half empty whereas Annabel's and Lucy's were usually half-full or even overflowing at times. Peter had been more of a mix of the two and David missed his balancing presence in the family.

"How was your day Georgia?" David asked.

"Alright I guess," replied Georgia who was slowly tucking into her curry with her head down.

"Was the gym busy today?" asked Lucy.

"Not really," replied Georgia, who was not one for speaking long sentences or offering lengthy descriptions. Annabel rolled her eyes towards her as the rest of the family jointly observed Georgia's downbeat state.

"You've not had anything odd happen to you today like we have then Georgia?" asked Annabel.

"Nah, not really. Although there was one weird thing though – in the pool around lunchtime." She worked at the local leisure centre just a mile away as a personal trainer. Georgia was, despite her regular lack of energy, a fitness fanatic who'd always wanted to work in the health industry. She'd been a prominent swimmer at her school and had always kept herself fit and healthy – which didn't always match her personality.

"Go on – what happened?" said Annabel, who was now tucking into her curry too.

Georgia didn't look up and continued to eat her curry, speaking with her mouth full, which always irritated Annabel. "Well, it was about half 12 and the alarm went off, so we all had to head for the pool. A child had got into difficulty and the mum who was with the little girl had panicked and screamed for someone to help. Tommy had dived in from the lifeguard's platform and pulled her out. She was fine though."

"Sounds quite dramatic," said David.

"Nah, not really Dad, but she said something really weird when we got her into the first aid room."

"Sounds interesting," said Annabel, now fully engaged in Georgia's story.

"Yeah, she said a man helped her under the water. The poor kid was only six years old, but she was convinced a man had lifted her up out of the water. When her mum asked her who the man was, she said he was an old man with white hair. Tommy is as bald as anything – he doesn't have any hair at all, but when her mum told her Tommy had rescued her, the little girl got quite upset and insisted it wasn't him. But there was no-one like that in the pool at the time, so we don't know who she was talking about. We just assumed she'd got confused."

"Well it's a good job Tommy was on hand then wasn't it? Could've been a lot worse," said Lucy.

"Yeah, I guess so, and what was even funnier though was that at the end of the session, when everyone was out of the water, we found a red sock – in the deep end of the pool. It was just floating in the water as if someone had dropped it there. No-one came to claim it, so we put it in lost property. Maybe someone will claim it next week. Very odd though."

David had stopped eating his supper. "Are you OK love?" said Lucy. "Is the curry OK?"

"No, it's fine, I was just a little taken aback by Georgia's story," said David.

"I know. Tommy must've felt like a hero," said Lucy.

"It happens all the time Mum," said Georgia, downplaying the excitement the rest of the family may have been feeling.

"Thanks for putting the card on Peter's stone too love."

"That's OK Mum. It was nice to go and speak with Peter."

The meal continued with bursts of conversation and moments of silence only broken by the sounds of buzzing mobile phones which were placed (under house rules) away from the kitchen table while they ate.

Once everyone had finished their curry, they all helped stack the dishwasher and clean the kitchen, before the girls once again returned to their bedrooms to continue their virtual social media lives through their phones.

"We've all had quite a day haven't we David?" said Lucy.

David was tapping his fingers on the table and seemed lost in thought.

"Yes Lucy, it's been a very strange day. But it's been a good day hasn't it?"

"Yes love, maybe it is time for some hope to return to our lives," said David.

5.

David slept well. He hadn't enjoyed a deep relaxing night's sleep for a long time, so when the alarm went off, he was surprised to see the clock showing 6.30am. He quickly turned back the duvet and slipped out of bed, picking up his jogging trousers, top and training shoes, before tiptoeing out of the bedroom.

He went to the bathroom to use the toilet and got dressed. As he descended the creaking stairs and headed for the door, he wondered who he was going to meet on his walk. Yesterday had been an incredible day. Despite being a sad day remembering Peter's birthday, it had been full of strange coincidences, synchronicities and encounters with unusual people, and that gave him hope.

The early morning light was pushing through the crack under the front door and David stepped forward to turn the latch. As he got to the door, he could see something just sticking through the letterbox. He pulled out an envelope, but in the gloom he couldn't make out who it was for. He turned and grabbed his jacket from the bannister and pushed his arms into each sleeve, swapping over the envelope. Turning back towards the front door, he gently opened the latch to let some light into the hallway and then returned to the bottom of the stairs, sat down and started to put on his training shoes ready for his walk. He put the envelope down onto the stairs next to him and the morning dawn just afforded enough light for him to see the envelope fully. It was bright red and on the front was written in neat letters – 'There is nothing in here – it's for you to fill. My suggestion is to fill it with love.'

The word 'love' was underlined as if to emphasise its importance.

The envelope wasn't sealed and there was nothing inside. David turned the envelope over a few times, looking for some sort of clue as to who had pushed it through his letterbox. He wondered if Mary, the vagrant he'd met on his walk, had placed it there, or perhaps Michael, the old man from the park bench.

He sighed and folded the envelope in two, placing it inside his jacket pocket, where his hand touched the medal he'd carried in his pocket the previous day. He took out the medal and placed it into the envelope so he wouldn't lose it.

He stepped out of the front door and gently closed it behind him. The day was grey and cloudy, and the morning light didn't pierce the early morning mist.

As David headed down the drive towards the park, he wondered who he might meet on this morning's walk. But by the time he'd reached the park gate, there had been no milkman, no strange vagrant encounter and there was no robin on the gate to meet him. He pushed open the gate and walked briskly into the park, determined to raise his heart-beat and get some warmth into his body. He quickly passed the park bench where the previous day he'd met Michael, and headed towards the cemetery. As he reached Peter's headstone, the roses and cards placed there the previous day were all still in place and David stopped.

"Morning Peter, I had the strangest day yesterday, of all days. You'd have loved some of the coincidences. You were always talking about coincidences. Well, I had a belly full yesterday." David leant forward and touched Peter's stone. "See you later, big man", he said, and he stood up and continued his walk through the cemetery, passing the chapel where he'd spent time with Samuel Hutchinson.

He felt warm and full of energy as he began to walk back around the far side of the park to complete his return home. As he reached the farthest point from home David noticed the park was a little untidy. Bushes seemed more unkempt and the pathways had grass growing over the edges. It was as if the park wardens didn't tend this part of the grounds as carefully. Maybe it was because it was further from the cemetery and less people used this part of the park.

David heard a rustling from one of the bushes in front of him and he wondered if a bird or animal was going to emerge. He stopped walking. The park felt silent, even though in the faint distance David could still hear the melody of the London morning traffic. The bush quivered as if holding onto the creature it was hiding and then suddenly a man stumbled from behind the bush, startling David, who stepped backwards involuntarily.

"Bore da!" said the man in a thick Welsh accent. He was wearing a green boiler suit, green wellington boots and green cap, all of which were dirty and appeared to have seen better days. The man had long brown sideburns protruding from underneath his cap and his face looked weather-worn, as if he'd spent most of his life outside. His cheeks were rosy, and his eyes were a bright green, almost matching his outfit. David noticed a wheelbarrow just behind the bush, with a spade and fork leaning against them. He realised the man must be one of the gardeners who tended the park.

"Are you OK?" asked David, concerned the man may have hurt himself as he staggered from the bush.

"Oh, I'm splendid thank you," said the man. "George Jones, park gardener," and he thrust out his hand to shake David's hand.

Instinctively, David put out his hand to shake George's large hand. "Morning George, you startled me a bit there."

"Sorry about that. I was busy pruning the bush you see."

"You're starting work early today aren't you?"

"Ah yes, but there's always weeds to attend to boyo. They grow like wildfire if we let them you see. We must keep on top of them, particularly in this here part of the park where people don't pass through often. It's easy for weeds to grow by here you see."

David instantly liked George. His strong Welsh accent suggested he hadn't been in London long or he'd certainly spent most of his life a long way from the capital city of England.

"Whereabouts are you from George?"

"I'm from all over the place me, but I've found my home here. When you're a gardener you see, you go where the gardens grow and that's all over isn't it my boy?"

David was puzzled by his answer but drawn into his jolly demeanour.

"What were you doing with the bush then? This part of the park seems a little overgrown doesn't it?"

"Oh yes, this is the part of the park where few folks come to, you see. That's why the weeds grow strong here. You must tend to the weeds you see or eventually they'd take over and before you know it, the whole park looks like this by here."

George took off his cap and scratched the top of his head, which was completely bald except for a narrow strip of dark brown hair around where the base of the cap would sit, which then extended down into the long sideburns. It was just as if by removing his cap, his hair came with it. He replaced his cap, adjusted it and then turned back to David.

"Right then young David, are you a gardener?"

David paused. He couldn't recall giving George his name but then dismissed the thought. "No, not really, my wife tends to take care of our garden. I'm too busy to get involved to be honest."

"That's not good my boy. You've got to tend to your garden all the time or else it gets overgrown." He cocked his head to one side and looked at David as if assessing him. Peculiarly, it reminded David of the robin the previous morning.

"Look down there," he said, pointing away from them both back towards the cemetery and the chapel. "No, not there... there!" he said, ensuring David knew exactly what he was pointing at.

David looked in the direction of George's arm and all he could see were more paths, bushes, grass and weeds.

"Can you see it just beyond the small cherry tree on the right? See the pathway through there. It was almost gone until I started to clear it. Tragedy it would've been if we'd lost that pathway."

David didn't really understand why it was important or why George was being dramatic about this one pathway.

"That's the pathway to Hope though boyo. If you lose that one, you lose all the other paths."

David turned towards George who was now leaning on a fork about six feet away. He felt unnerved and a little spooked as George had moved quickly and quietly. He was pointing to where the fork was penetrating the ground.

"Look by here my boy. See this small weed here. It's called Bellis perennis. But you know it as the humble daisy. You see, it can look quite pretty, as if it's going to bloom into something wonderful, but it never can grow into something truly beautiful. That's because it's actually a weed and eventually, if you don't dig it out, it will take over and all you'll see is daisies. In fact, the whole park would be covered in them you see. We dig them out quickly or else there'd be nothing else by here other than daisies."

David hadn't expected to be receiving a horticultural lesson on his morning walk and he was beginning to regret stopping and looking at the rustling bush. He sensed George might be lonely and enjoyed chatting to passers-by about his gardening.

"Being a gardener is an important job you see David. 'Cos if you neglect your garden, weeds will grow, and Hope is lost."

That word 'Hope' again. It was like a chiming bell in David's mind, taking him back to the previous day.

"But it's easy to remove the weeds David. All it takes is a bit of love. That's all boyo."

George was smiling and he winked as if what he'd just said was supposed to be something David would recognise as important. David didn't recognise it at all. He didn't like gardening and was beginning to think about moving on and leaving the gardener behind.

"But everything starts with Love, doesn't it now?" said George. "If you want something to be better, you throw a little love on it don't you boyo?"

A car horn blasted in the distance, momentarily taking David's attention away from the strange gardener.

"Er...maybe."

"Come over here boyo", and George motioned for David to follow. David wanted to finish his walk and get on with his day. He decided he wasn't keen to spend more time with this stranger, who seemed keen to teach him about his gardening techniques. George began walking behind the bush and past his wheelbarrow. David followed, even though his mind was screaming at him not to.

George walked a few paces in front of David towards a hedge. As he arrived at the hedge, he stepped straight through it, clearly knowing the hedge wouldn't hurt him or prevent his progress. When David arrived at the hedge it looked impenetrable.

"Come on boyo. Just step through the hedge," George called from the other side. "If you don't step through the hedge, you'll never get to see what I need to show you. Come on now boyo. You can do it."

David stood in front of the hedge, which looked like a hedge in his own back garden. One of the very few tasks he would undertake in the garden was to trim hedges and cut lawns and this one looked like a privet hedge – dense and tough. There was no way he could simply step through it.

"But if you don't try to step through it, you'll never know what it looks like on the other side, will you?" called George, clearly getting impatient.

David put his hands into his jacket pockets as if to make himself feel smaller and stronger. One hand touched the red envelope with the medal of 'Faith' inside it. He shut his eyes, turned his shoulder towards the hedge and took a deep breath. He pushed forwards and was instantly through the hedge and on the other side. When he opened his eyes, he gasped. In front of him was a beautifully tended lawn leading up to a small church. There were numerous grave-stones dotted around but each was perfectly maintained and clean – unlike the main cemetery where many of the stones had been left to fall into disrepair and ruin.

George was standing in the doorway of the church, which was simple in construction with a single tower and nave. David's knowledge of history was poor so he couldn't date the church, but he noticed the lack of ornate stone carvings. Whilst it was a simple looking church, it felt almost magical to David. Its simplicity was its beauty, drawing David in and pulling him towards George, who wore a broad smile.

David looked around and could see the hedge he'd stepped through encircled the church, meaning it was completely enclosed as if in a secret garden. He walked towards George and noticed that the constant noise of the London traffic had disappeared completely. The silence was slightly eerie but also felt somehow comfortable and safe.

"The silence is important David," said George.

"Where are we and why is there no entrance to the church through the hedges?"

George removed his cap again and reached into his pocket. He pulled out a handkerchief and wiped his head, removing some perspiration. He placed the handkerchief back in his pocket and turned to David.

"Look by here," said George, pointing to a wooden plaque above the entrance to the church. It was a simple plaque with some words inscribed onto it which read, 'Abandon hope all ye who enter here'. But the word 'Abandon' had a line drawn through it and above it someone had written by hand the word, 'Restore'.

David recognised the phrase 'Abandon all hope ye who enter here'. It came from a poem about entering through the gates of hell. David shivered and wondered what was behind the door into the church.

"This is the place where us gardeners come. Only us gardeners know where to find this place you see boyo. It's where we come to restore hope when all is lost. You don't even need to step inside this here church. It doesn't matter what's inside here, it's just you need to know this place called Hope exists in your garden too."

David was confused. He wasn't sure why George had brought him to this place to stand outside a church. Once again, he thought about returning to his walk and getting on with his day. But there was something intriguing about George and the church and the fact that the place he'd brought him to was somewhere in Waterlow Park he'd never discovered before, even though he'd lived and worked in this area all his life. No-one had even mentioned the church behind the hedges before, so he was curious to know why he'd never found it and why George had appeared in the park on his walk.

"Come over here," said George, who started to walk around the church towards a small wooden bench amongst the well-tended gravestones. He sat down on the bench and started to remove his wellington boots, revealing thick woollen socks. He waggled his toes and rubbed his feet. "Ah that's better. Nothing better than taking off your boots at the end of a hard day is there boyo?"

David sat next to George on the bench. "The day has only just begun George!"

"Oh yes boyo, for you maybe but for us gardeners, we're often working when you're fast asleep."

David wondered if in fact he was dreaming, and he would wake up and discover himself lying next to Lucy. But George felt real and the church was real. For the first time in a long time, life felt real for David.

"Is all this real or am I dreaming?"

George laughed. "It's all real alright boyo. And real is what you want your life to be isn't it?"

David did want it to be real and not just a strange dream. He wanted more of his life to feel as real as this did, sitting with this jolly Welsh gardener.

"OK my boy, listen here well then. You see, the thing with gardening is, it starts with some silence. That's why folk love their gardens and why we find them peaceful. It's often where we can find some silence and it's in between the thoughts the head gardener speaks to us."

"The head gardener? Who's that?" asked David.

"You know. The gardener who helps you think and feel everything David. Where do you think your thoughts come from? The best thoughts are often found in the silence and that's where the head gardener works best."

David looked down at the lawn in front of him and considered what George was saying. "I'm not sure what you mean? When I spend time in silence, all I get are horrible negative thoughts about how I've been a total failure, how I've let down my family and how they'd be better off without me. That's why I avoid silence or meditating or anything weird like that."

George scratched his chin. "Mmm, yes, I can see that boyo. That's because the weed planter occupies the same place. He loves to fill up your garden with weeds that choke and destroy the plants that truly want to grow. That's why you need to fill up your garden with the plants, trees and flowers you dream of. And to do that, you simply start with Love."

David remembered what the writing on the red envelope in his pocket had said and he reached into his pocket to show George. He couldn't find it. He realised it must've fallen out of his pocket as he pushed through the hedge. It also meant he'd lost his 'Faith' medal too. His heart sank.

"But I don't love gardening, I've already told you!"

"It's OK boyo. You don't need to love gardening, but you do need to find what it is that you do love to do. Finding real happiness starts with Love you see boyo and whilst your garden is full of weeds it's very hard to see the things you love. But they are there, often in the quietest parts of the garden. It's like this church, you had to push through the hedge to find it, just like breaking through the wall of noise occupying most of your life outside this park. If you can find the hedge, you can find the church. And if you can find the church, you can find Hope. Just remember that David."

George started putting his boots back on. "Must press on now boyo. I need to get that bush trimmed before someone catches themselves. Thorny bushes need to be carefully tended or else they get out of hand, don't they David?"

David's head was full of questions about the head gardener, the weed planter and the idea that he had to find what he loved to do to find happiness. All David had been trying to do for the past five years was to build a business which would deliver a secure lifestyle for his family and in this he had completely failed. Finding happiness in what he 'loved' to do didn't make sense.

"Come on now," said George standing up. "Let's get back to the day and start looking for the things you love David." He walked back towards the place where they had come through the hedge, but as they got closer, there was clearly a gap in the hedge with a small, black iron gate.

"That gate wasn't there before was it?"

"The gate was always there David but when your head is full of weeds, you just can't see it."

George opened the gate and invited David to step through. "I'm stopping here for a while. I just need to gather some more tools as there is a big tree on the other side of the park which I need to trim."

He offered his hand towards David. David took it and they shook hands.

"It's been a pleasure to meet you George. Thank you for showing me this special place and I hope to come back and see you again."

"Oh, you'll see me again boyo, you can be sure of that." George turned and walked away from David back towards the church. He lifted his cap, just as Michael had done the day before.

David shut the gate and walked down a short path back to the main pathway. He turned back to where the bush had been to see if George was still there. David noticed that the bush where they had met was a rose bush and just at the tips of the bush were small red roses.

David smiled and turned back towards the main pathway and his journey home. The morning traffic was noisy, and he realised just how much background noise existed that he hadn't noticed before. He decided he would need to find more peace and quiet in his life to work out how he could do more of what he loved. He wasn't sure what this meant but he knew he had to focus on planting positive thoughts into his mind after so many years of listening to the weeds that had grown. He chuckled as he walked along and understood what George had given him. As he came to the usual gate at the exit of the park, he heard the familiar sound of the robin he'd heard the day before. The little bird was sitting on the gate chirping away merrily. As David pulled on the gate to pass through, the brave robin didn't move.

"What've you got in store for me today then mate?" asked David. The robin just continued to chirp merrily at him, clearly doing what he loved to do.

As David headed back towards the house, he felt a buzz of excitement. He wasn't sure what he loved to do but he knew he had to spend some time finding out. His body tingled and it was as if something new had been planted inside him.

As he got back to the house, he placed his hand inside his pocket to find his key. His hand touched something else: the envelope. He pulled it out of his pocket and could feel the medal inside too. He realised he hadn't lost the envelope or the 'Faith' medal at all. They had been there all the time.

He read the words on the envelope again.

'There is nothing in here. It's for you to fill. My suggestion is to fill it with love.'

He pulled out the medal and turned it over. David gasped. The word on the medal was 'Love'.

6.

David stood motionless on the doorstep to his house, with the medal in one hand and the red envelope in the other. The sun was rising in the sky and pushing through the grey clouds. The day seemed brighter somehow than previous days. Or was it just his mood?

He turned the key in the door and stepped inside, quickly removing his training shoes to avoid walking grass or dirt along the hall. His socks left moisture marks on the hard floor as he walked down towards the kitchen where he flicked on the light switch and headed towards the kettle. He filled it, clicked the on switch and then sat down at the kitchen table where the previous evening the family had shared their stories of their unusual day. It seemed today was going to be another unusual day and he wondered what was happening in his life. Just forty-eight hours ago, life had been a mess. Finances were tight and the family were faced with losing their home. Business was tough too, and he'd felt exhausted and washed out.

Nothing had changed in his circumstances and yet to David, it felt like something else was beginning to change. The people he'd met in the last two days had given him a new sense of hope and faith that life was going to work out. It felt like a light was flickering where darkness had been present before.

The kettle boiled and clicked off. David watched the steam emerging from the spout into the room. It quickly disappeared and he wondered if his new sense of optimism would disappear just as quickly. He smiled and remembered what George had said. A weed was about to grow in his mind, so he quickly dismissed the thought.

He stood up and poured the boiling water into the empty teapot next to the kettle, adding a couple of tea bags from a jar. He could hear Lucy stirring above, as the floorboards creaked and then the sound of running water could be heard as she turned on the shower.

David sat down at the kitchen table again and looked at the red envelope and the medal he'd placed in front of him. He wondered who had pushed the envelope through his front door and how the medal had switched to 'Love'. He also thought about the church in the quiet part of Waterlow Park which he'd never found before. He wasn't ready to explain to Lucy all that George had told him or anything about his encounter with the mysterious gardener. The text above the church puzzled him too. *'Restore hope all ye who enter here'* was the unusual text above the door of the church.

"Morning Dad!" It was Annabel, as cheery as ever and heading for the kettle. She was wearing her purple fluffy dressing gown and big slippers in the shape of two large hamburgers. Her hair was sticking out at right angles from her head and she shuffled around the table barely awake. "Have you made some tea?" she asked, tapping the side of the teapot to see if it was hot.

She came around the table and sat down opposite David.

"You look rough," said David, slightly amused by the dishevelled state of his eldest daughter.

"I feel rough Dad. I was awake half the night with crazy dreams. Really weird stuff too."

"Oh yes," said David, "what sorts of weird things?"

Annabel leant forward towards him moving swiftly into her more dramatic persona, delighted she was going to be given the opportunity to tell a story.

"There were lots of things Dad, but one of the weirdest dreams was about this church and how it was hidden by tall trees and no-one could find it. But I'd found it Dad and it was beautiful."

David leant towards Annabel too. "A church eh? What did it look like?"

"Well it wasn't that pretty. It was quite ordinary really but there were two men standing outside the church talking. I couldn't see who they were, but I felt safe and like I knew them. You know how it is in dreams Dad, nothing makes sense. But I really wanted to go into the church, like it would be peaceful and quiet if I did. As I walked towards the two men the door opened in front of me and I stepped into the church."

David's hand gripped the table in front of him. "What was inside the church then?"

"Oh, I don't know," said Annabel. "I woke up just as I entered the church, but I wasn't scared Dad. And it felt real." Annabel got up and shuffled around the table towards the teapot. "Shall I pour the tea Dad?"

David didn't answer, he was still taking in what Annabel had said.

"Dad! Do you want some tea?"

"Er...yes please."

Annabel grabbed a couple of cups, added some milk from the fridge and stirred both cups with a teaspoon pulled from the drawer next to the sink. She placed David's tea in front of him, took a sip from her own cup and then began to shuffle towards the door.

"There was one other thing I remember from my dream," said Annabel, pausing in the doorway. "It's a bit odd, but as

I was about to enter the church, one of the two men at the doorway turned to me and said, *'Love is always the place to start'.* But he had a very odd accent; Irish or Welsh or something. It was just after that when I woke up. I wonder if I'm going to meet my prince eh Dad?" Annabel chuckled to herself and left the kitchen, shuffling her burger covered feet along the hallway and up the stairs.

David sat motionless, staring at his cup of tea which Annabel had placed in front of him. Something strange was occurring in his life and he couldn't explain it. Maybe he didn't need to explain it. Maybe he just had to accept the strange similarities as nothing more than coincidences. But Annabel's dream was very odd and too close to his own experience to be dismissed as coincidence. It was as if she'd been observing what he'd been doing. It was all a bit too surreal and exciting for David who preferred the comfort of thinking life was hard, and that he was worthless. He caught himself again and recognised the weeds he was planting in his mind.

David smiled and decided that whatever was happening to him and whoever was being sent to help him, he'd listen. He'd find some silence to tend to his mind too as he realised just how easy it was for him to put negative thoughts there. He realised it was a habit; comfortable and familiar. But he knew he had to begin to pull up some of the weeds in his mind that George had talked about and to maybe break through the hedges in his own comfort zone.

"Morning."

David turned around the see Georgia fully dressed and in her running gear. "Are you going for a run?"

"No Dad, I always wear my running gear in bed."

Sarcasm was one of Georgia's habits, but it made David smile. He also knew he wouldn't get much more than short sentences out of her, as she wasn't a morning person like Annabel.

"OK, enjoy your run," he said.

"I will," she replied, putting her headphones into her ears as she exited the kitchen.

David started to think about the day ahead. He'd got a supplier coming into the depot to talk about new ranges. He disliked salespeople as they were always too cheerful for his liking. They talked in riddles, trying to convince him their product was going to save his business. The person coming in was of the worst kind – young, ambitious and full of himself. Smart-suited and going somewhere, he epitomised everything David disliked about business. Whilst he was trying to make ends meet and keep his staff employed, this young upstart was simply trying to build his career without a care in the world. He wondered if they took salespeople on some course to teach them 'blind optimism' as they all seemed to carry the same disease.

"Morning honey," said Lucy as she entered the kitchen, fully dressed and ready for her day. Lucy worked in a branch of Langham Solicitors in Muswell Hill, just over a mile away from their house. She'd always worked there, with nearly 20 years of unblemished service, and had only worked in a couple of their branches too, all within a few miles of where they'd lived. When the children were small, she'd worked part-time, slowly building her hours as they got older. Lucy didn't like change, so she'd been entirely content to work in the same place, doing the same job (she worked as a cashier) for the same employer. The only break she had taken was when Peter had died and even then, she'd only taken a week's compassionate leave.

"Morning. Did you sleep well or were you having strange dreams like Annabel?"

"Slept like a baby actually – I didn't even hear you go out for your walk this morning. How was it? Did you meet any strange characters like you did yesterday?"

David paused and wondered whether to tell Lucy about George and the hidden church. But it all sounded a little too far-fetched in his mind now, so he dismissed the idea. "No, it was pretty uneventful today," he said. "Anyway, I'd better get showered and ready for work."

"Would you like me to do you some breakfast while you're in the shower?" asked Lucy.

David stood up from the table and walked over to Lucy. He held her shoulders gently and planted a kiss, softly onto her cheek. "I love you," he said.

"Blimey, your walk must've done you good this morning. I can't remember the last time you started a day with an 'I love you'. But I love you too honey, now get off and take your shower or you'll be late for work." She waved her arms at him to encourage him to leave the kitchen and he duly obliged, heading up the stairs and straight into the bathroom.

As he showered, David wondered why he'd felt he wanted to tell Lucy he loved her. He didn't really express his emotions well and preferred to 'show' Lucy he loved her by providing for her and buying her presents. He rarely told her he loved her, so he was surprised himself when those words came out of his mouth. Maybe he had filled up the red envelope with love after all and his chat with George had made more of an impact than he realised.

Once he'd showered and dressed, he returned downstairs to the kitchen. Lucy had put a bowl and some cereal out for him on the table and he sat down and began to pour himself some cornflakes. The small portable TV was on in the kitchen and Lucy was watching breakfast television, something else she did religiously every day including weekends.

David noticed the news headlines being broadcast and there had been another explosion in a big city in Egypt, killing many and injuring even more. It seemed every day, the TV news would report more tragedy, more destruction and more despair. David found it very depressing and didn't understand why Lucy would start her day with the world's collapse being broadcast into their kitchen.

"Gosh this is depressing Lucy. Must we watch this every morning?"

"Oh, don't be silly honey. You're always saying that. It doesn't depress me anyway; it just makes me even more grateful for what we have."

David admired Lucy's ability to contextualise the world around her. Annabel certainly got her optimism from Lucy, and between them, they were like a pair of positive batteries, sparking off each other all the time. Their world was rosy, pink and fluffy, even though they both liked to watch the news, or worse still, documentaries about the poor nations of the world where children were starving, or a country was ravaged by war. They would sit and "ooh" and "ah" as the programmes unfolded whilst Georgia and David left the room to watch something else on another of the numerous televisions they owned.

"I just find it all so depressing," said David. "Why can't we all just live in peace and harmony? And why are we cruel to each other? It makes no sense at all."

Lucy was busy preparing her lunch for the day and had her back to David. "It all makes perfect sense to me honey," she said. "You can't have love without hatred, and you can't have light without the dark, can you?"

David wasn't sure what she meant, and it sounded a little like something she'd read somewhere in one of her self-help books he despised. In his view, books suggesting life could be better, rosy or even hugely successful just by changing your thoughts or action, were simply fanciful. But if it made Lucy feel better, he tolerated her occasional outbursts or quotes of psychobabble.

"Yeah, whatever you say Lucy. Where did you read that one anyway?"

Lucy turned around to face David with a short, sharp knife in her hand she was using to prepare some salad for her lunch. She waved it at him. "Look, just because you choose to believe the world has gone to pot, I don't want to. And I didn't read it anywhere. It's just obvious to me you can't know what love feels like unless you've had periods in your life when love isn't there."

David felt a little guilty. "Is that why you were surprised when I told you I loved you this morning? Have you felt that there have been times when I haven't loved you?"

Lucy returned to her salad preparation as if not wanting to answer David directly, or at least look him in the eye when she responded. "Yes, there have been times when I wondered if you still loved me. I always sort of knew you did, but it's been hard when you've been down and depressed. It's as if a big wide space opens between us and it stops us connecting. When you tell me you love me, it fills that space and makes me feel re-connected to you. I really value that because of the times when I haven't felt it – does this make sense?"

"OK," said David, although he wasn't sure why or how it made sense. He just felt it was best to agree with Lucy and close the conversation down, as it was a bit heavy for a pre-work breakfast chat.

"I was reading something the other day that made sense of this though David."

"Oh yes? Which super-duper self-help book was this then?" David's sarcasm, shared by Georgia, was often used as a defence mechanism when he felt he was on the back foot.

Lucy turned around again, but this time had her arms by her side in a much less threatening stance.

"The author said that for every action, there had to be a reaction. For every positive, there had to be a negative. For every good there had to be a bad. Essentially, you can't have one without the other, as they are two sides of the same coin. For instance, if we didn't have night-time, we wouldn't know it was daytime. If we didn't have sadness, we wouldn't know what it felt like to have joy. He said, if you were simply happy all the time, you wouldn't know you were happy. You must have some context to allow you to truly feel all the emotions and learn about the world. It made sense to me anyway. So, although things are a bit rough for us now and we're short of cash, when it does come back, as I know it will, we'll appreciate it much more. Do you see what I mean David?"

David was nodding. "But it doesn't mean you need to watch depressing news programmes all day does it?"

"They are only depressing if you choose to see them that way," said Lucy. "I see them as another way of giving me context and appreciation of what we have. I don't get depressed, I feel grateful. Gratitude comes from recognising what you have. This means you must experience an element of not having the things you desire too."

David was beginning to feel like he was in some sort of therapy or coaching session, but he decided to drop his resistance. "OK love, I hear you. And I'm sorry if I don't tell you often enough how much I appreciate you and love you. You know I do love you, don't you?"

"I do now," said Lucy. She walked over and kissed David on the cheek.

"Yuk," said Georgia walking back into the kitchen from her short run. "Get a room you two!"

David and Lucy laughed. "OK hon, I'm off now, have a good day and I'll see you later."

"Cheerio then. Hope you have a good day too!"

David left the kitchen and headed down the hallway towards his day and his appointment with the sleazy salesman. As he reached the door, he remembered the envelope he'd found sticking through the letter box just an hour earlier. The writing on the envelope had talked about filling it with love and he smiled as he realised that the conversation he'd just had with Lucy was all about love. And maybe he needed to experience a lack of love to truly appreciate what he had.

By the time David arrived at the depot, he'd stopped thinking about love. He was focused on the day ahead and just how he was going to pay the staff salaries. There was a supplier payment run due too and Melissa, who was the part-time accounts clerk, would be wanting to pay their various supplier accounts on time. She'd be expecting David to sanction everything, but he knew there wasn't enough money in the bank to pay the salaries and the supplier accounts, so he'd need to ask Melissa to prioritise the salaries and leave some of the supplier accounts unpaid. Melissa wouldn't be happy. She had been a bookkeeper all her working life and she prided herself on her efficiency, honesty and integrity. When a bill was due to be paid, she liked to pay it within the payment terms of the supplier. Postponing payments made her feel very uncomfortable and so David wasn't looking forward to the look of disdain he knew was coming his way.

As he entered the small car park at the back of the depot, he could see Melissa's car already in one of the spaces. Promptness was also one of her values. He parked his car in his own parking space and switched off the engine and got out of the car. As he pushed the door shut and pressed the switch on his remote-control key, he looked at his ten-year-old Jaguar X-type. When he'd bought it, it was a huge achievement and one his personal ambitions fulfilled.

Growing up, he'd dreamed of owning a Jaguar car, so when the business was flying, he purchased with cash a brand-new Jaguar X-type in metallic blue, with full leather interior and all the whistles and bells you could throw at a car. He felt he'd truly arrived, but ten years on the car looked a little like David felt – old and tired. The alloy wheels had been bumped and scraped, there were scratches down the sides where various mishaps or brushes with trees and bushes had taken their toll, and the interior was fading and looked worn. David chuckled as he realised the car was a perfect description for how he felt about his life.

"Morning guvnor," said a voice behind David. It was Eric, the longest serving member of staff at the depot. Eric was his father's first employee and he'd worked in the business for nearly forty years. At sixty-eight years old, he should have retired a few years back, but he loved coming to work and would wash cars, do deliveries when drivers were stretched or help in the yard unloading and loading delivery trucks. Eric simply loved being at work and had no intention of retiring, and so David hadn't the heart to ask him to leave. But with money tight, Eric was someone the business couldn't really afford to continue to employ.

"Morning Eric – how are you today?"

"Well the sun's up, my Tom Jones ain't aching today and there are plenty of folk out there that'd love to be in my place, so life is good me old china plate."

Eric was always cheerful. Since he'd lost his wife a few years back, he'd decided retirement wasn't an option, and now he was a bundle of cockney charm every day. His demeanour never wavered, and everyone loved him. It pulled at David's heartstrings when he thought about asking him to retire because he could no longer afford his meagre wages.

"See the jam jar is still looking great. She's a real beaut' ain't she? Always dreamed of having a Jaguar me, but I guess

I've never got to the crazy heights you've achieved, have I?" Eric slapped David on the back with genuine glee and a hint of sarcasm.

David realised he'd been looking at his car and seeing it as a reflection of his poor status and performance, and yet Eric was viewing it through envious eyes. A pang of guilt swept over David and he wanted to have some of Eric's passion and optimism.

Eric started to walk around the car. "Would you like me to give the old girl a little spit and polish guvnor? Looks like she could do with a bit of love, don't she? You don't want her to feel like she ain't important no more do ya?"

David felt even more guilty. "Yes, that would be great, Eric," and he handed Eric his keys.

"Don't you worry guvnor; I'll have her looking all sparkly in no time."

Eric headed towards the large hose kept in the corner of the yard and he whistled a nondescript tune as he went.

David walked the short distance to the back of the depot, through the double doors and onwards to his office. There were already a couple of customers at the trade counter and Billy, the young apprentice, was serving them. "He'll be another casualty," thought David as he headed into his office.

As he walked behind his desk to sit down, Melissa entered the office. "Morning David, can I have a quick word?" David knew it wouldn't be a quick word, as Melissa would want to go through in full detail whatever was on her mind.

"Sure Melissa, how can I help?"

"Well, I've just come to pay the salaries and there isn't enough money in the main account to pay them. I've checked the other two accounts and they are close to empty too. It looks like the cashflow problem I identified a couple of months ago has indeed come true and now I can't pay the salaries today. I've also checked the debtors list and whilst there are only a few large payments due this week, there still won't be enough to pay everyone. I'm worried David, as we've been close to the edge before but never this tight. Your father would never have let things get this bad you know."

This final remark cut into David and whilst it seemed a low blow, it came from a loyal and long-serving employee who had also started in the business when his father was alive and in charge.

David sank into his chair and put his head in his hands. He heard the office door shut and looked up. Melissa was sitting in the chair in front of him. She was in her sixties, but she had taken good care of herself and looked about ten years younger. Having never married, she had had an active outdoor life where she had travelled extensively around the world on her holidays and was always experiencing new things and new places. David had often yearned for her sense of freedom to do and go where she pleased, and her well-journeyed lifestyle had created a wisdom and sincerity David admired. Therefore, when she spoke he listened, even if it did cut into him like a knife.

"I'm not sure we can make it through this time Mel," said David. "I'm really worried about what I'm going to do."

Melissa reached across David's desk and touched his hand. "David, there are times when you need to make tough decisions in life. But if you pray about them first, you'll always get the guidance you need. God is always there for the big decisions in life."

Melissa was a committed Catholic who was a regular at St Joseph's parish church in Highgate, just on the edge of Waterlow Park. Religion had simply not offered any concrete answers to David's challenges in life. However, as he'd told Samuel Hutchinson, he did possess some sort of belief or faith in a higher power and maybe Melissa was right that the only answer to the problems at TPS was with the 'Gods.'

"Thank you, Mel, but this is serious. I've put as much cash as I can back into the business and whilst the banks have been helpful recently, the salary run must go ahead today or else I'll have mutiny on my hands. I don't know what to do."

"Let me have another look at the payment schedules. I could possibly postpone a couple of supplier payments today, move a little cash around in the various accounts and we might just be able to run the salary payments. Plus, I don't mind waiting a week or two for my wages David. I know it won't make a huge difference but every little helps doesn't it?"

"Mel, you're an angel. I don't know what I'd do without you. Thank you for all you do for me."

"That's fine David. Let me do what I'm good at and what the good Lord called me to do too. It will be OK, don't worry. I'll come back in a little while and tell you what I plan to do once I have worked it all out."

Melissa got up from the chair in front of David and walked out of his office. With her glasses perched on top of her smartly groomed grey hair, she looked the epitome of efficiency.

David wondered how she could be so positive and practical. Her ability to carefully work the business through tight situations had been a genuine gift to David over the years and he'd relied on her skills and talents many times.

David could hear Eric whistling in the car park and he wondered how he could be so positive, especially since losing his wife after forty years of marriage. In Eric and Melissa, he recognised people with passion and skill for what they did. It was humbling for David that two such loyal people were now at threat due to his inability to lead and manage the business through the troubled economic times the country was facing.

The phone rang on his desk and he picked it up.

"David Turner," he said somewhat abruptly.

"Morning Mr Turner, it's Billy here. There is a gentleman here to see you. He says he has an appointment. His name is John Benjamin and he's from Smithwood Piping. Can I send him through?'

Billy was coming on well. At just seventeen years of age, he'd become one of the best apprentices David had employed in a long while. Bright, polite and passionate about plumbing, he had real promise and David was very proud of how he was developing. "Yes, send him through, thanks Billy."

John Benjamin was the young, enthusiastic salesman David was dreading seeing, as he'd clearly been to the 'never take no for an answer' school of sales and 'everything is brilliant' school of sales phrases. He was overly positive and passionate and not at all what David felt like enduring.

There was a knock at his office door followed by the door opening, even before David had the chance to invite him in.

"Good morning David, how are you?" John thrust out his hand and shook David's hand with an iron-like grip and with vigorous handshaking. "It's a cracking day, isn't it? I went for my jog this morning and I thought to myself, today is going to be a great day!"

"Take a seat John," said David, trying to dampen John's enthusiasm a little.

John sat down and immediately started rummaging through his large pilot case which always contained something he couldn't wait to show David.

"How's business then David? Booming, I hope? We don't need to participate in this recession, do we?"

David's heart sank further, and he wasn't sure if he was going to be able to stomach a visit from this over-optimistic and falsely enthusiastic salesman. And of course, the standard "How's business?" question always had to be answered with a lie.

"Good thanks John. I don't have much time this morning so could we crack on?" Avoidance was always the best tactic to steer the talk away from how the business was really going.

"Great to hear David, great to hear. There are many merchants out there struggling David, so it's good to know there will still be some businesses for me to call on eh?"

"Er yes, I guess so John."

"So many of the businesspeople I meet just don't seem to have the passion for their products, their customers or themselves even. Right bunch of misery guts I can tell you. That's why I like coming here David. I met Eric in the yard and he's like part of the furniture and he always has a smile on his face. He clearly loves what he does and that's what it's all about isn't it?"

David was thinking that love wasn't the answer to his salary run, although he did like the fact John liked coming to his business.

"Let me tell you about a new fitting we've got coming out in May this year. It's a new type of push-fit plastic fitting with a watertight guarantee and by that I mean it's guaranteed not to leak." John winked at David, another irritating trait of positive people who seemed to think winking was some secret sign that all was well with the world.

"We don't really need any new plastic push-fit ranges John; we've already got two ranges in stock." David knew John wouldn't take no for an answer. He'd try to unravel his objections, come up with clever ways to merchandise the products in the depot and he'd not give up until he left with an order. David had half a mind to simply ask him to leave but there was something about his positive outlook which felt curious to him. Nothing seemed to phase John, and whilst David was faced with not being able to pay his employees, he sensed that, faced with the same challenge, John would somehow find a way to overcome it.

After a few more minutes of discussing push-fit plastic fittings, David agreed to take a small range on trial and signed an order pad John thrust in front of him.

"It's great to do business with someone who is as passionate as me about what they do, David," said John with glee and a beaming smile.

"Can I ask you something John," said David.

"Sure. Shoot."

"How do you stay positive when you must get rejection during the day and not everyone is going to like what you sell. And I'm guessing many won't buy now as trade is bad?"

"That's a good question David and I'm happy to tell you. I haven't always been positive you see. It really began a few years back when I was out of work, having just lost a job I hated and had done for nearly ten years. I'd struggled to be successful and although I managed to meet my targets, I didn't like what the business stood for or how it was run. Their values simply didn't match my own and I struggled to do things the way they wanted me to. I remember one time we changed a range by reducing the quality a little, but we didn't reduce our prices or tell our customers. I felt uncomfortable and I just didn't believe in the company or its product ranges anymore. I stuck it out for a while, but they began to struggle and eventually I got made redundant. It was a real low point in my life."

"Gosh, I didn't realise that had happened to you John."

"No need to be sorry David, it was the best thing that could've happened to me. You see, I went on one of these career evenings and I met an interesting chap. His name was Michael and he told me he was just at the event to help.

I couldn't get him to tell me which company he worked for, as he said it wasn't relevant, but he gave me some simple advice which changed my life."

"Sounds interesting John, what did he say?"

"It was quite weird really, as he said if I wanted to be truly successful, I had to start with love. I'd never heard someone talk that way and he talked to me for about an hour about how people were looking for success in the wrong place. He told me I had to start with love and love was where I'd find my purpose again."

David's mind was stirring; some of what John was saying felt familiar. "Was the chap an older guy? Smartly dressed? I think I may have met him too."

"Yeah, he was, really smart but he looked like he should've retired really, rather than still be working or at a careers event. Have you met him then too?"

"I'm not sure John but tell me more about what he said to you."

"He talked about finding my purpose, which was a bit of a puzzle to be honest. He told me real success was something I had to 'feel' and not just 'do'. I'd always thought if I worked hard at what I did and became the best salesperson at my company, I'd be successful and enjoy all the trappings success brought, but it didn't work out that way."

David was very curious. "Did he explain what he meant by your purpose?"

"It was fascinating, David, and it changed my life I can tell you. He said I had to find four things: something I was passionate about, was good at and that enabled me to live out what I stood for. He also said I needed to feel some sort of connection or calling to what I was doing. It all sounded a bit unrealistic to me at the time but the more I thought about it, the more it made sense. He called them the four pillars of purpose."

"What else did he say?"

"He just asked me lots of questions, David. It was all a bit weird, but it really got me thinking about success and what I really wanted from life. He told me if wanted real success, I had to start with love and not with setting goals. It was the opposite of what I'd been taught in my sales training and it was the opposite of what most business and success gurus had said. But when he explained the importance of having goals built on love, it made complete sense. I've not looked back since."

"Did you get a new job, then?"

"Yes, I did and that was the other really weird thing David. At the careers event, there were lots of companies looking to promote what they did, desperate for new recruits. It was in the boom-time remember, when construction was vibrant and there were more jobs than people to fill them. I could pick and choose whoever I worked for really. But Michael told me to go home and work on my purpose before I looked for a job. But just as I was saying goodbye to him, I heard a commotion behind us, and someone had knocked a glass of water all over the table in front of one of the company's exhibiting and it had clearly ruined some of their leaflets and information. Michael walked over and took out his handkerchief and started mopping up the water. I followed him and pulled out my own little bag of tissues I carry with me and we were both dabbing at the water whilst the employees of the company were still arguing over whose fault it was that the water had been spilt. Michael then turned to me and said something I've never forgotten. He said, *Focusing on what's gone wrong never puts things right. Focus on what you are passionate about, good at, stand for and feel called to do and you'll always be able to cope with what life throws at you.* I've always remembered this and it's how I live my life now. I love what I do and I'm good at it. I like what my company stands for and its values fit with mine. And I know I am meant to be a salesperson. I couldn't imagine doing anything else. Have a guess who's been salesman of the year for the last three years David?"

John winked again, but this time it didn't offend David.

"I'm guessing you've been top salesman John?"

"You bet sir. Top salesman for the last three years and it's all because I followed what Michael said. It's funny, as after we'd been helping to clear up the spilt water, Michael told me he had to go, and he left. I had a question for him I'd forgotten to ask, so I asked around to see if other people had seen where Michael had gone but no one had seen him leave."

"What was your question?"

"He said that life was upside down and back to front and that we need to turn our lives inside out to really find true happiness. I wasn't sure what he meant, but I'll never forget my meeting with him, and I hope one day I'll meet him again."

David was uplifted by the conversation with John and it was extremely unexpected. He'd been dreading seeing John, as he knew how positive he'd be but now, having listened to the background to his story, he valued and enjoyed the time they'd spent together. It was in fact, entirely back to front, inside out and upside down.

"John, thank you for sharing this with me today. I think it was just what I needed to hear. To be honest, things in the business are pretty tough now and I've been wondering how to get us out of a pretty tight situation."

"Gosh David, you surprise me! I'd always assumed things were going well, as you always seem so positive. Maybe it would be good to remember what Michael told me. Focusing on what went wrong never puts things right does it? It's easy to blame yourself, look backwards and think you could've made better decisions. But I'm sure every decision you've made in the past you made with the best of intentions. We rarely intend for things to go wrong, do we? Perhaps it's time to look forwards and not backwards. Is there anything I can do to help?"

"I'm not sure John, but I know you're right about one thing. I've never done anything or made any decisions in the past to deliberately make things worse. Everything I've done has been with the intention of making things better, but I guess some of my decisions weren't right in hindsight."

"Ah yes, but hindsight can be a waste of time and energy David. We can all look back in hindsight and think we could've done something differently. But the key is to use hindsight to develop wisdom. Doing the same thing again we know didn't work is just ignorance. But doing something different in the future with the benefit of hindsight is wisdom."

"You've a wise head on young shoulders John," said David, admiring the clarity and wisdom with which he spoke.

"I don't think age makes a difference David. I've met many people much older than me who are stuck in a rut they could've got out of many times. And to be honest, a rut is just a coffin with the ends pushed out anyway. Why live your life in a coffin? I made a decision after I met Michael to live my life with purpose and I've not looked back since."

"Gosh, you truly are an inspiration mate," said David. 'I've been sitting here this morning worried about paying salaries, but I've realised I've been focusing on the wrong things. In fact, I can see I've been allowing weeds to grow in my garden too."

John looked confused. "Weeds in your garden? What do you mean?"

"Oh, it's OK, it was just something someone said to me this morning when I was walking in the park. He was a gardener and he told me I had to be careful to pull up the weeds of negativity in my garden or else they'll take over my mind. I can see I was allowing myself to do this before you walked through my door this morning."

"Great analogy. We've all got weeds in the gardens in our minds David. How about I try to help you with a solution this morning? I'll speak to our finance team and ask them to increase your payment terms from thirty days to sixty days for the next three months. That will buy you some time and reduce your outgoings a little and mean it's one less invoice for you to pay. And I'll also add the new range we agreed this morning on a sale-or-return basis, which means you only pay for what you sell. Will that help?"

David wasn't used to suppliers offering extra credit or sale-or-return deals. He would usually beg and insist on such offers and yet here was John, offering them to him.

"That would be amazing John but surely, you'll have rules and you can't just give extra credit away so easily can you?"

"Being the top salesman David gets me the credibility and trust from my director and the finance team, which I can use to help important customers like you. We know it's tough in the market, but we want to help. It's one of the values of the business I really like, and it chimes with me. I know if I help you now, it will build our relationship and greater trust between us and that's better for everyone isn't it?"

"It's certainly an example of you doing things upside down and back to front! I've never been offered extra payment terms before. I usually need to ask! Or should I say 'beg'!" David laughed out loud and it felt good. "I really appreciate your help John – I genuinely do."

John felt good too. He loved his job and loved to help people in difficulty. He liked David and enjoyed visiting Turner Plumbing Supplies. "It's a pleasure David. If there's anything else I can do, just give me a call."

"I will, and thanks again John." David suddenly felt a pang of guilt for feeling negative about John's visit. He'd been so wrapped up in his own negativity he'd already judged John even before he'd walked through his office door. But he'd misjudged John and perhaps his own situation. Maybe there *was* a way forward. Maybe he just needed to step forward and do what he was good at, which was being in front of customers. Maybe he had to get out from behind his desk and start making things happen.

A knock on the office door interrupted his thoughts and he looked up to see Melissa standing behind the office door. David waved for her to come in.

"Hiya Melissa," said John turning around with a big beaming smile.

"Morning John, can I just have a word with David?" she replied in her usual efficient manner.

"Sure, do you need me to leave?"

"No, it's OK," replied Melissa. "I just wanted to let you know David, we'll be OK regarding the discussion we had earlier."

"Great news Mel," said David. "John's aware of our predicament so it's OK to talk. He's offered to help us with some extended payment terms too."

Melissa cast a look towards David, suggesting she was surprised he'd shared delicate financial information with a supplier. Forever the pragmatist, Melissa felt that certain elements of information should be on a strictly 'need to know' basis and in her view, she classified John, a young upstart who spent most of his time in the depot laughing and joking with the staff, as a definite 'not needing to know' about the finances of the business. She struggled to hide her frustration at David's apparent willingness to break some basic protocols.

"Oh, OK," she said. "I just wanted you to know I completed the cashflow and managed to move a few things around, and we'll be OK with the situation we discussed earlier." She was also irritated John had stolen her thunder somewhat as she was looking forward to telling David she'd solved the cash-flow problem and yet this young salesman with his flashy suit and even more flashy smile had got in before her.

"That's great news," said David, trying to reassure Melissa he did appreciate her efforts.

"Fine," was all Melissa said and she turned on her heels and pulled the door to behind her with a force designed to demonstrate her discontent with being trumped by the young salesman who everyone else in the branch seemed to like, but to her was far too optimistic and positive for her liking.

"Oops, I think we may have upset your finance lady," said John, breaking the slightly awkward atmosphere.

David laughed again. "It's fine John, I'll talk to her later. I'm just glad the day is looking far better than I anticipated about an hour ago."

"Yep, it's all about digging out those weeds David. A negative attitude will hardly ever solve a problem but a garden full of positivity can be a garden full of possibility!"

"Cheesy line," said David, smiling warmly at the young salesman in front of him.

John smiled back. "Cheesy but true David. I'll get out of your hair now and make a few phone calls to set up the revised payment terms. I'll come and see you next month and we'll review how things are with you. It's been great to see you." John began to close his pilot case and was getting up from his chair.

"Just before you go John. The old chap you met; did you notice anything strange about his attire? Was there anything out of place, like something that didn't seem to fit?"

"You mean his red socks? Oh yes, I spotted those when we were chatting. We'd sat down for a while and I couldn't believe he was wearing these bright red socks when everything else about him seemed to be perfectly tailored and groomed."

"Yes, you've definitely met the same Michael as I have. How strange! What a coincidence!"

"There's no such thing as coincidence," said John. "Michael told me that too. He said there is only synchronicity, and everything is working to a plan. I wasn't too sure what he meant but I think it was no coincidence I came to see you today David."

"I agree John. I really do appreciate you coming in. I'm going to be thinking about my four pillars of purpose, which seems an interesting place to begin the journey to more success. Thanks for sharing it with me."

John put out his hand and David shook it warmly. The young man then placed his other hand on David's shoulder.

"One last thing Michael said to me David. It was when he caught me looking at his bright red socks. He simply said, 'Nothing is perfect is it?' and I knew what he meant. I'd been focussing on what had gone wrong in my life rather than what was going right or could be better in the future. I urge you to do the same my friend."

David felt a wave of emotion come over him as he looked at the young man called John who stood in front of him. He realised that John was just a few years older than Peter would've been. "Thank you, Peter," said David.

"Peter?"

"Sorry, John, I was just thinking of my own son, who you know we lost. You reminded me of him. It was a slip of the tongue that's all."

John looked deeply into David's eyes. "I'm touched David and I'm sure if Peter was here, he'd be proud of everything you've achieved. It's time to look forwards and not backwards now."

"Thanks again John, I really appreciate our time today."

"It's been a pleasure David. See you in a month's time and you know where I am if you need me."

John turned and left the office and David watched him walk through the depot, waving at staff and joking as he went. Eventually, he disappeared through the door on the far side of the depot and was out of sight. David returned to his desk and pulled out a pad of A4 paper which was sitting on top of a pile of papers waiting for filing, a task he detested and avoided. On the top of the pad he wrote the word 'Love' and underneath he drew four vertical lines. At the bottom of the four columns he'd created, he wrote the words 'Passion,' 'Talents,' 'Values' and 'Calling'. Then he wrote 'The four pillars of purpose' at the top of the page, underlining the phrase four times.

It had been a strange morning already and it was only eleven o'clock. He'd met a mysterious gardener in the park and had now had a meeting which had unfolded in a way he hadn't expected, with someone he hadn't even wanted to see. He'd begun by thinking he'd be forced to lay off some of his most loyal employees and now he was sitting at his desk knowing he could pay the salaries and no-one would lose their jobs, for the time being at least. It was certainly a back to front, upside down day.

David leaned back in his chair and thought about the last few days since he'd met Michael in the park, and he shivered as if someone was watching him. He instinctively turned around and looked straight into the eyes of his father in the picture on the wall behind him. The picture had been taken at a gala dinner when he was recognised for his contribution to the plumbing industry. He looked smart in his dinner suit and David knew it was one of the proudest moments in his life.

"Am I making you proud Dad?" David asked.

"Every day," was the reply from a voice inside his head.

7.

The rest of the day had flown by. David had sorted the cashflow with Melissa and organised how they would get through the next few weeks. He'd even got Melissa to call a few of their other suppliers to ask for some extended credit terms and each one had obliged either in part or in full to their requests.

As David walked back towards his car, he could see Eric had been hard at work, as the car gleamed. Eric had a passion for perfection, and he would have spent far longer on the job than he probably needed to. But it was a trait David admired. He was clearly very good at cleaning cars, as the interior was spotless. David thought about John's visit in the morning and their conversation about passion, talents, values and calling, and he realised that, in many ways, Eric's work on his car had been an example of all four pillars of purpose. It was why he just couldn't lay Eric off. He had to make the business work so Eric could continue to live his life of purpose through the business, even though he knew Eric would have volunteered to work for free as he loved his job so much.

As David drove the short distance to his home, he thought more about his purpose and his own life. Plumbing had never been something he'd been truly passionate about, even though most of his life had been surrounded by piping, tubing, central heating boilers and taps. His father had simply assumed he would follow him into the business and whilst he'd been proud of his father's achievements, he'd never shared the same passion for the business his father had maintained until he retired and even then, he would regularly pop in to chat to the boys on the trade counter or have a chat with Eric.

David wondered what he was passionate about. He enjoyed seeing people develop in the business and enjoyed having meetings with other business owners, but he couldn't think of much else to get excited about.

As he pulled into the drive back at the house, Lucy was in the front garden tending to some of the plants in the flowerbeds. She was kneeling, so she got up and wiped her brow with her wrist. David got out of the car and grabbed his briefcase from behind his seat and closed the door.

"How was your day honey?" asked Lucy.

"Very interesting actually Lucy. I had a visit from that young salesman John who comes in every month which really did turn my day upside down and inside out." David chuckled to himself.

"What's funny?" asked Lucy, standing with her hands on her hips.

"Oh nothing, it was just something John said. The garden looks lovely, have you been out here long?"

"No, just a little while. I noticed some of the plants had weeds around them, so I thought I'd just come out and have a little tidy up. Can't be allowing those pesky weeds to take over, can we? I was reading something in my book this morning and it said successful people do all the tiny things unsuccessful people can't be bothered to do. I decided to come out and do some weeding as I know many folks wouldn't bother."

David smiled. "Sounds like an interesting idea Lucy, what's the book you're reading?"

"It's all about doing the little things that make a big difference and doing them consistently. We might not see a benefit now but if I keep on top of things in the garden by regular bouts of small activity, hopefully we'll see the benefit in the summer."

David loved Lucy's positive outlook on life. Maybe her personal development books weren't such a crazy idea after all, and the idea of doing something small, important and consistently was something David recognised he hadn't been doing with the business or perhaps in his life. He preferred bursts of activity and would often notice things that needed to be done but would then put them off or ignore them completely, only to pay the price later.

"Would you like a cup of tea love?" asked David as he headed towards the front door which was slightly ajar.

"Oh yes please, I'd love one. I won't be long. I'm just going to complete this weeding and then I'll be in to start the dinner."

David walked into the house, along the hallway and into the kitchen. He filled the kettle with water and flicked the switch. On the table were two books Lucy must've been looking at. One of them was '100 Tips to Make Your Garden Weed Free' by someone called George Jones.

The kettle clicked off as the water boiled and David sat down at the table. He flicked through the pages of George's book and there were photographs of hundreds of weeds and ways to kill them off and stop them spreading. There were also tips on how to keep your garden looking beautiful all year round, including the weeding Lucy had clearly decided to do.

As David sat holding the book by George in his hand, he wondered if it was the same George Jones he'd met earlier in the park.

"Where's this tea then David?" said Lucy as she walked into the kitchen.

"Oh sorry, I haven't made any. I got distracted by the books on the table. Where did you get the books from honey, particularly this one about gardening?"

Lucy took off her gardening gloves and pulled out another chair from around the table, which scraped across the floor. She sat down flushed but ready to tell her story. Like Annabel, she loved telling stories and this one had been a real puzzle to her.

"Well it's really odd David. I was walking back through the park this afternoon after a really challenging day at work. I'd had an awkward customer give me a hard time on the phone. I felt down about my job and as I was walking through the park, I was thinking, maybe after all these years at Langham's it's time to step away and let someone else do my job. They've offered us the chance to apply for voluntary redundancy you see, and I was thinking perhaps I was getting too old for the job and it needed someone younger."

"Gosh, you're only forty-six love, which you can hardly call old. You've got plenty of years left yet." David was trying to reassure Lucy but was also becoming nervous about the idea of her taking redundancy, as they relied on her salary to keep them afloat. Whilst the idea of a lump sum after her long service could be helpful to their cashflow, the loss of ongoing income was not something he wanted to consider.

"And that's when he appeared," said Lucy.

"Who appeared?"

"The gardener. As I was walking past the far side of the park, he just stepped out from behind a bush. Gave me quite a fright I can tell you."

"I think I met him this morning love. He did the same to me. But he's a jolly fellow, isn't he?"

"Yes, he was jolly enough, but I told him he shouldn't have jumped out in front of me like that, but he then said something odd. He said that sometimes in life, things do jump out in front of us, but we ignore them and move past. He said they were like a nudge or an intuition we notice but ignore. I was ready to move on past him when I realised maybe he'd jumped out in front of me for a reason."

"What did he say then?" asked David, bursting with curiosity.

"He just reached into the pocket of his overalls and gave me this book. He said that I had to mind the weeds in my garden, as if I let them, they'd take over. But if each time I noticed a weed, I pulled it out, I'd keep on top of my garden."

"It's definitely the same chap I met this morning. Did he show you the church?"

"You never mentioned meeting anyone this morning. Anyway, no, what church?"

"It's OK. He took me though some hedges to a church I'd not seen in the park before and I just wondered if he'd take you there too."

"No David. I wasn't likely to go off wandering through hedges with some chap who'd just jumped out of a bush in front of me. Are you mad? He could've been a nutcase or something!"

"But I sensed he wasn't love. Maybe it was my intuition as you call it, but I just felt he had something to say to me, so that's why I did go with him to the church he showed me which was in a beautiful and quiet part of the garden that I'd never found before."

"Well, although it was a bit strange meeting George, when he gave me the book, my instinct wasn't to give it back to him. I felt I had to keep it, which is very odd if you think about it. But it felt the right thing to do, so I simply said thank you and began to walk away. Then as I did, he said something even stranger. He said that the garden is a place where we can restore hope and that we should enter with care. I didn't know what he meant, and it gave me the creeps a little, so I just walked away. But I kept the book David and brought it home. And when I started to flick through the pages, I realised there were some interesting tips in it. If I'd thrown away the book, I'd never have seen some of the great tips I know can help me in my garden."

David smiled.

"What's funny?" asked Lucy.

"Nothing really. George is harmless enough and I think he meant to help you and probably to help me too. Maybe he thought I'd allow some weeds to grow in my garden and I needed to be reminded to remove them as they appear."

"You hardly ever help me in the garden David, so I can't remember the last time you pulled up a weed!"

David smiled again and looked at the book Lucy had placed back on the table.

It had been another day of surprises, coincidences and synchronicity. As Lucy began to busy herself preparing the meal for them all to eat, David sat in silence replaying the events of the day in his mind. Something was changing around him, but he couldn't place what it was. His world had been invaded by people who all had messages for him. Nothing seemed the same anymore and he wondered if he was just imagining the feeling building inside of him. His belief in the future was more optimistic, more hopeful and more exciting. He felt like his mind was clearer, cleaner and ready to accept what lay ahead.

David felt emotion well up inside his chest and he couldn't prevent a tear squeezing out of his left eye and running down his cheek.

"Are you alright honey? What's wrong?" asked Lucy.

"Nothing love, I was just thinking about my dad."

"He'd be really proud of you now, wouldn't he? You've managed to steer the business through some tough times David, and I know he'd be delighted you're still running it and working in it too!"

"I'm not sure I want to be in it or running it for much longer though. I was thinking today that it's never really been what I wanted to do. I just followed Dad into the business as it was expected of me. I'm not passionate about it in the way he was. And I'm not sure I'm good at it either."

"But you've kept it going through some tough times haven't you. And the staff love you, so you must be doing something right."

"I've always tried to run the business in a way I felt I'd want to work for a business. I guess my own values have been there but I'm not sure it's what I'm meant to be doing with my life now. Something John said to me this morning has really stuck with me. He said to be truly successful in life, you had to find your purpose, or you'll always struggle to 'feel' successful, even if you've appeared to 'be' successful. It really resonated with me and it got me wondering if it was time for a change."

"It sounds like we've both been thinking it's time for a change today then honey." Lucy was chopping vegetables and had her back to David who was still sitting at the table.

"Anyway, I'm going to pop upstairs to get changed before supper." David got up from the table, kissed Lucy on the cheek and headed towards the door. "Thanks for listening love."

"It's what we do honey. Us women are good listeners."

"I know," said David. "But thanks all the same."

As David climbed the stairs, he could hear two different types of music coming for the girls' bedrooms. Annabel was singing to some cheerful pop tune whilst Georgia was playing her guitar. Both had different preferences in music, and both certainly had different talents. Annabel could sing but had never picked up an instrument whilst Georgia couldn't sing at all but had been fascinated by the guitar from an early age and was now an accomplished rhythm guitarist, playing with a small local group. The idea that they each had their own passions and talents struck David as he went into the bedroom to change.

David noticed more books on Lucy's side of the bed. There was always a pile of personal development books, novels, magazines and her iPad sitting on her bedside table. For years, Lucy had read books and attended courses she felt made her better, happier and more content, despite never actually changing her career. She would invite David to attend some courses with her, but he'd never agreed, always criticising the idea that someone else could help you develop. In fact, he'd even accused some of the speakers and gurus Lucy had followed as leaches who fed on the discontent of their audiences.

But for some reason he felt through one of those nudges or intuitions that he should go over and look at Lucy's latest collection. As he walked around the bed, he noticed a magazine on the bedside table called 'Be the Best' and it had a picture on its front cover of a speaker on a huge stage with his arm punching the air as the audience waved their arms and appeared to be cheering.

David picked up the magazine and realised it was just a small six-page brochure promoting an event being held near Birmingham called 'Be the Best'. Inside the brochure there were articles, quotes and details of speakers who were going to be at this event and how, if you were serious about personal development, you 'had to be there'. Some of the quotes and copy made David squirm, as there were promises of 'transformation,' 'personal growth,' 'spiritual enlightenment' and 'unrivalled success' bursting from every corner of the brochure. Does anyone actually believe this stuff? David thought to himself.

He put the leaflet back on Lucy's bedside table and made a note to ask her about it when he went down for supper. After changing into some jogging bottoms and t-shirt and placing his clothes from the day into the laundry basket, he headed back downstairs to find Lucy. The smells of another curry were emanating from the kitchen and David felt his stomach rumble. He'd not eaten all day and he was ready for whatever Lucy had prepared.

As he entered the kitchen, Lucy was just serving the curry into bowls.

"Can you call the girls please David."

David turned back out of the kitchen and shouted upstairs to tell the girls their supper was ready. They both acknowledged him, so he returned to the kitchen to quiz Lucy about the brochure.

"What's the brochure about upstairs love?" he asked.

Lucy continued to serve up the curry, spooning rice and counting. "Which brochure honey?"

"The one about the event called 'Be the Best' being held near Birmingham. You know, the one with all the speakers and gurus you love to read about."

"Ah yes. Rosie told me about that, and I thought it looked quite interesting. One of the speakers is Robin Anton, and Rosie says he's good. Lots of people have been to his events and their lives have been changed, so Rosie asked me whether I wanted to go with her. Would you mind?"

David didn't mind at all, but he did think it was a waste of time and money, which was something currently in short supply. "What do you think you're going to learn though love? You'll just end up spending money and the guru gets richer and his audience just gets poorer!"

Part of David wanted to know more about the event, but he'd built up such a resistance over the years, so he was unable to shake off the feeling that such events were just a huge money-making exercise by the speakers at the expense of people who desperately wanted success, but who couldn't afford their ticket prices and went home worse off than when they arrived.

"You're such a cynic David. How can you ever learn anything new if you believe you know it all already? A shut door means you never get to see the secrets which lie behind it. I just wish you'd come along sometime and see the people there are not charlatans, cheats or dream stealers. Some of the speakers are often people like you who've been through hard times and then tell their stories to help others. I think it sounds really inspiring, and I'd like to go."

Lucy began to place the curry on top of the rice she'd just placed in the bowls. But the way she was throwing the curry at the bowls, David knew he'd riled her with his cynical comments. And deep down, he *was* curious. But the skin he'd been wearing for so long was difficult to shed. He'd not wanted these speakers to be right, because if they were, he'd wasted much of his life doing things he didn't enjoy, he wasn't particularly good at, often in a way that didn't sit comfortably with him and most certainly he didn't feel 'called' to do. If these speakers had the answers, why wasn't everyone doing what they loved, were good at, stood for and were called to do?

"I'm sorry love. I wasn't meaning to pour water on your fire. Tell me more about it."

The curry was now served up and Lucy sat down, calling out, "Girls, your tea is going cold on the table!"

Georgia shuffled into the kitchen and sat down without saying a word, quickly followed by Annabel who skipped around the table, pulled out her chair and sat down with a whoosh.

"This looks lovely Mum. Chicken curry – my favourite."

Annabel's enthusiasm for everything in her life was something David had always admired. It was as if nothing could burst the bubble of positivity she surrounded herself with.

"What's up with you two?" asked Georgia with her typical directness.

"Nothing Georgia," said Lucy. "Just your Dad being a cynic as always."

David sighed. He didn't want to be cynical. He wanted some of Annabel's optimism and Lucy's openness to possibilities. "It's OK girls, Mum and I were just talking about an event Mum wants to go to."

Annabel put down her fork. "Do you mean the 'Be the Best' event in Birmingham we were talking about yesterday Mum? It sounds great doesn't it Dad?"

"Waste of time," mumbled Georgia with a mouthful of curry. There was something comforting and familiar to David in Georgia's consistently pessimistic and downbeat outlook. He would often end up siding with her in an argument.

Lucy was clearly still annoyed and was becoming more irritated, pushing her curry around her dish and not actually eating any. "Look, just because I think learning new things and stepping outside your comfort zone is a good thing, I don't see why you two must be so cynical and negative. We are all adults in this family, and you can choose to do what you want to do but don't stop me from doing what I want to do."

"Blimey Mum," said Georgia. "No need to go off on one."

"I'm not going off on one. But just because I've worked in the same place for a long time and just because I cook and clean for you lot, doesn't mean I haven't got dreams you know. And we all owe it to Peter to make the best of our lives. He didn't get the chance..." Lucy's voice trailed off and the room fell silent except for the chink of cutlery and crockery as they ate in silence.

Annabel broke the uncomfortable atmosphere. "I'll come with you Mum if you'd like someone to go with."

The atmosphere lifted a little. "Thanks Annabel, but Rosie has offered to take me, so I'll just go with her thanks." Lucy had clearly decided she was going to attend the event, whether David approved or not.

David stirred his curry around his bowl, feeling guilty that his own cynicism had put such a dampener on Lucy's enthusiasm for something clearly important to her. He remembered how he'd felt on the way into the depot earlier in the morning and how John had lifted him with his positivity, his talk of purpose and his willingness to help, and yet he was not offering his wife any support at all.

"I'll come with you Lucy. We'll make a weekend of it." As the words came out of David's mouth it was as if someone else was speaking.

Lucy looked up from her curry. "You're just saying that because you feel guilty. I'd prefer to go with someone who genuinely wants to come. I'll go with Rosie thanks."

The room fell silent again but inside David, something was stirring. It felt like he was on the edge of a cliff waiting to jump and he suddenly felt dizzy. He grabbed the side of the table.

"Are you OK Dad?" asked Georgia.

"I'm fine thanks." But he didn't feel fine at all. He felt like he was being pushed in the middle of his back and he felt cold. There was a tightness in his chest, and he suddenly didn't feel hungry anymore.

Annabel had put down her fork and was staring at David. "Blimey Dad, you've gone really pale. Are you sure you're OK?"

David felt like he was on a rollercoaster and a roundabout all at the same time. The room was spinning, and he felt like he couldn't keep his eyes open. Then the pain in his chest started to travel down his arm. He put down his fork.

"Ring an ambulance Lucy," he managed to gasp.

Annabel stood up from the table. "Mum, quick, Dad's not well."

Lucy looked over at David and he was shivering. "What's the matter honey?"

David knew what was happening.

He had watched his father die. He knew he was having a heart attack.

"I love you," was all he could say. And then everything went black.

8.

David could hear a strange sound in the distance. Like an alarm going off but it was a soft bleeping sound.

He opened his eyes and could see bright lights above his head. He lifted his head and his eyes focused. Suddenly Lucy's face was in front of him.

"Lie back honey. You're safe. You're in the Whittington. You've had a heart attack love. Just lie back."

David put his head back onto the pillow. Everything seemed fuzzy and he couldn't remember what had happened, how he'd got to the hospital or why he was lying in a bed wired up to a series of machines making various bleeping noises. He could hear voices, but everything was in the distance. Then someone touched his hand.

"You scared me Dad. I thought you'd died." Georgia was holding his hand on one side of his bed. He turned his head to see his Annabel staring at him. She looked awful.

"You can't leave us yet Dad. We've got too many exciting things to do!" He realised both daughters were holding his hands, something that hadn't happened since they buried Peter.

"Where's Mum?" asked David.

"She's chatting up the dishy consultant over there," said Annabel, pointing towards the middle of the ward which David was slowly beginning to recognise.

David looked towards where Annabel was pointing and noticed there were beds either side of him and three beds opposite where his bed was situated. It was a small side ward of six beds and all of them were occupied and surrounded by machines bleeping and flashing. Two men were sitting up in their beds opposite him whilst one man was sleeping. Either side of him, two more men were sitting up in their beds with headphones on their heads and they were both watching the televisions hanging from the ceiling.

The two men opposite also had people around their beds talking quietly.

"Welcome to Hanger One mate," said the man to David's left. "Looks like you've had a Sean Connery like the rest of us then?"

David was just waking up and his brain hadn't clicked into gear. And then it slowly began to dawn on him. He was in a coronary ward. He'd obviously had a heart attack.

"Er... yes, I guess so."

"Antony Giles, although most people call me Tony. Good to meet you me old china."

"I'm David, David Turner. Good to meet you Tony. How long have you been here?"

"Ah, just a couple of days mate. Had me a Sean Connery at work. Had to bring me in with blue lights an' all. It's me second one you see. I didn't change nothing after me first one, so I've been given a whole load of grief by the trouble and strife. Gotta change now yer see or it's goodnight for me mate."

David was still drowsy and the chatter from Tony was a bit too much for him to deal with. He was lying in a hospital bed and yet the last thing he remembered was sitting in his kitchen discussing an event Lucy wanted to attend.

"I'll leave you to your family then David. Gotta go for me oily rag anyways. Me Missus tells me I should stop but it's one of me last pleasures you see. If I can't have a smoke, then I might as well give up all together eh?" Tony started to climb out of his bed and picked up a packet of cigarettes and headed out of the ward.

"How are you feeling honey?" asked Lucy who'd returned from her conversation with the consultant.

"Not too bad love, but my chest is a bit sore. What happened?"

"You just keeled over at the table. Georgia had to catch you. The ambulance was with us in a few minutes, but they were the longest few minutes of my life. You gave us a right old scare. It's time for us to rethink some things love. The doctors say this was a mild heart attack and it needs to be a warning to you. They're going to do some more scans and want to check to see if your valves are all working OK, but you should be out tomorrow or the day after. Then we're going to sit and have a good chat about life and what we want from it. I really thought I was going to be facing the second half of my life alone."

Lucy reached down and squeezed the hand Annabel was still holding.

"I'll be fine," said David. "I need some rest and then I can get back to work. Just a little setback that's all."

"It's a bit more than a setback Dad," said Georgia who was leaning back in her chair. As pragmatic as ever, she was about to give her dad both barrels. "You've got to change your ways Dad. There's no point in just sitting there thinking this is a setback. Jesus Dad, you nearly left us."

"And we really aren't ready for that yet Dad, you know that too," said Annabel. 'I've never been so frightened in my entire life. It was horrible waiting for the ambulance. You can't put us through that again."

David looked around at his family. The gentle hum of voices in the ward, along with the bleeps and buzzes of machinery, all seemed to fade into the distance as everything important to him was sat around his bed. He knew his life had to change. He'd been feeling it for the last few days and his encounters in the park and even with people coming to see him at work had all started to affect his thinking. In fact, he'd felt more positive than he had for some time and yet, here he was, lying in a hospital bed having nearly lost his life.

"I know. Don't worry, I'll slow down a little at work. It's been a tough time recently, but I will slow down, I promise." As he said the words, he felt the promise was as much to himself as it was to his family around him. Something had to change, but as he lay in his hospital bed, having just survived a life-threatening event, David had no idea how to change. He'd always been a driven and ambitious person who wanted to succeed and enjoy the trappings of success – they'd all enjoyed periods when life was good. The past couple of years had been much tougher, but David had reasoned they were tough for everyone, as the economy had been going through the biggest recession since the second world war.

"Mr Turner, it's time to review some of your life choices."

It was the dishy consultant who looked young enough to be still at school.

"I'm Raj Patel and I'm the senior registrar for Doctor Sharma, your consultant."

Raj spoke without a hint of accent and David was struck by the warmth and tone of his voice.

"Hi there, what's the prognosis then doc? Am I a lost cause?"

"No, not at all. You've experienced a very mild myocardial infarction which may have damaged your heart muscle, so we need to check your heart is still working OK and all your valves and arteries around the heart are working as they should be. But I think you've had a lucky escape Mr Turner and you should take it as a warning sign to reduce your stress levels, watch your diet and slow down a little. Has anyone from the cardiac rehabilitation team been to see you yet?"

'No, they haven't, but I've only just woken up, so I don't know if they've been round when I was asleep." David looked around at Lucy to see if she knew if anyone had been to see him.

"Actually, a nurse did say that a dietician and a physiotherapist would come round but we haven't seen them yet. Is there anything we need to do as a family, doctor?"

"The only thing you need to do is to get your husband and your dad to slow down. Men of his age are prime candidates for heart attacks and strokes, but they rarely listen to us until it's too late. Get him to think about his work and how he can reduce his stress levels and get him to up his physical activity too."

David didn't like the fact he was being talked about as if he wasn't there, particularly by someone who looked young enough to be his son. "OK you lot, I'm capable of looking after myself. I don't need you all mollycoddling me."

Raj was writing some notes onto the clipboard hanging from the end of his bed and appeared to have ignored David's comments.

"Right then David. I'll see you tomorrow when hopefully we can discharge you but for now, get some rest and I'll ensure the cardiac rehabilitation team come around to see you today." He then moved away from the bed and out of the ward.

"Phoar, he's a bit of a dish, isn't he?" said Annabel, lightening the atmosphere.

"Yes, he could bring his bedside manner to my room any time he likes", said Georgia in an unusually light-hearted way.

"Yes, he is rather nice isn't he," added Lucy.

"Blimey you lot, leave the poor kid alone, he's young enough to be a toy boy for all of you!" said David. "I can't believe how young some of these doctors are to be honest."

A bell rang in the distance signalling the end of visiting hours.

Lucy stood up and leaned towards David. "I'll come back this evening honey, you need to get some rest now and we'll all come back later." She kissed him on the forehead and began gathering her handbag and coat. Georgia and Annabel both kissed him and said their goodbyes. Within a few minutes, the ward had cleared, and David was left with his fellow patients and the nursing staff for company.

"So, me old china, what d'ya do for a livin' then?" It was Tony again who'd returned from his smoke.

"I run a plumbers' merchant business Tony, how about you?"

"I'm a postie mate. Have been all me life. Wouldn't have it any other way neither. Fresh air, exercise and just the birds for comp'ny. Even when it's pouring down, I love my round. Worked out of Holloway sorting office for the past 27 years and the whole time, I've had the same round. I know every house, every street and every name and address. It's like they're me extended family if you like. And I'm happy being on me Jack Jones ya see. Happy in me own comp'ny. How about you then David, do ya love yer work?"

David was struck by the simplicity and honesty with which Tony spoke. He'd clearly had a simple approach to work and had managed to find contentment and happiness in his life. David was envious but wasn't about to reveal this to his new friend.

"Yeah, I do enjoy it sometimes. There's lots of pressure and business has been hard for a few years but I keep on keeping on. You know how it is."

But David wasn't sure if Tony did know how it was to struggle. He was clearly a big man; as he sat up in his bed he still looked as if he was tall and broad. He was wearing blue striped pyjamas and had a tattoo of a swallow on his neck. David suspected he had more tattoos on the rest of his body too. He guessed he was about fifty, from the very small amount of hair on his head. He'd shaved his head to avoid looking bald and his scalp and face were weather-worn and clear evidence of his outdoor life.

"Do ya love yer work then boss or not?"

It was quite a direct question which David thought he'd answered already.

"Yes, I do enjoy it most of the time."

"Nah, you ain't gettin' it me old china. You gotta love yer work, not just enjoy it. 'Cos if ya love yer work, yer work loves ya back, do y'see?"

David didn't see or wasn't keen to continue chatting to his cheery cockney companion. He was tired and slightly bored of Tony's simple approach to life. But Tony was unperturbed by David's lack of enthusiasm.

"Ya see, my old man bought his chips when he was just forty-four. Worked all his life to make things good for us he did. Worked himself to the bone to try to give us more stuff. But all we wanted as kids was to spend more time wiv him. But then he went and bought it just around the corner on Highgate Hill. Tragic it was. And seeing him working all hours God sends and not being happy, made me realise happiness doesn't come in boxes or bags or in things. It comes in doing what ya love, which is why I stayed being a postie cos I love it ya see. And cos I love what I do, what I do loves me back by looking after me. I got me pension coming and I can spend more time down the bowling club with me mates, have a few jars and being as happy as a pig in pig shite. What more can a man want eh Dave?"

David was struck by the simplicity of this view on life, but he wasn't convinced it was possible to just love your work. You had to be ambitious and aim for more, so you can achieve more for your family.

"Do ya love what ya do my love?" Tony was asking the nurse who had entered the ward and was looking through the charts on the end of his bed.

"Of course I do," she replied. She was a short black lady who spoke with a strong Ghanaian accent David recognised. "I came to this country to be a nurse in your National Health Service and I love looking after my patients. All except you Tony. You're a right handful I can tell you."

Tony laughed. "You see David, this lovely lady came all the way over to our country to work here 'cos she loves it. You couldn't be a nurse if ya didn't love it could ya my love? Even the bacon sarnie who came round just now must love what he does, young bloke like that."

"I think Doctor Patel is from this country Tony, not from Pakistan," David said.

"Well whatever, it don't matter. What I'm saying to ya me old china is, these here folk don't get paid fortunes, but their fortune comes from somewhere else. Are ya getting what I'm sayin'? When ya aim for more simple things, ya end up with more. Like my old mother used to say, when you've got more, ya just want more. When ya aim for less, you'll always feel like you've got more."

What Tony was saying sounded familiar and David knew he'd heard it before from Michael on the bench in the park just a few days ago. Michael had said that accepting less didn't make you unhappy.

"Yes Tony, I hear you."

"I ain't sure ya do hear me mate. Listen. Look at this arm here." He pulled up the sleeve of his pyjamas to reveal a large tattoo which covered most of his forearm. David's hunch about his tattoos had been right. "And look here too," as he pulled up the sleeve on his other arm. There was another large tattoo which appeared to be in the style of a bird, perhaps an eagle. "These here tattoos cover up me scars. When I was a kid, I used to hurt myself ya see. I tried to top meself twice too. I just thought I wasn't good enough for me dad ya see. He wanted me to strive to be better, earn more money and do bigger things. But I just wanted to feel happy. After he passed, I had me tattoos done to cover up me scars. But underneath, they are still there. That's why I just do what I love now Dave. All I ever wanted was to see me dad happy, but he died feeling like he'd failed because he hadn't reached the place where he could feel happy with what he'd achieved. The graveyard at Highgate is full of folk who feel they've failed and I ain't gonna be one of 'em."

Tony turned away from David and for a moment David wondered if Tony was crying. It was painful to watch and hear, and he knew there was far more to this genuine cockney than David had first judged. He felt a pang of guilt as he realised he'd judged his cockney demeanour and jolly approach as childlike and naïve. Whereas the truth was, Tony had clearly been through some tough times and had come out the other side with a clear idea of what would make him happy. David realised he'd misjudged him before knowing his full story. He was envious of his new friend's clarity on life too.

"Thanks for sharing, Tony. I can imagine what it must've been like growing up with a father like that and I've realised listening to you, I'm a bit like your dad. I'd hate to think my girls look at me and think I'm expecting too much from them. Someone recently said to me I should reassess my life and my work so maybe it's time to do just that."

"Well there ain't any other time than now is there me old china?"

"No, I guess not Tony."

David lay back on his pillow and thought about what Tony was saying and realised he'd lived his life worrying about the future and regretting his past. The present was a time and place that David hadn't occupied much. As he drifted off to sleep, he wondered if the present moment was the greatest gift that most people simply didn't see or were aware of in their lives.

He closed his eyes and drifted gently off to sleep.

9.

When David opened his eyes, he could feel dampness around his mouth, as he'd been dribbling. He wiped his face with his arm and looked around. There was no-one around his bed and he remembered his family had left him at the end of visiting. He looked up at the large clock on the wall at the end of the small side ward and it said 11.11pm. The lights had been dimmed in the ward and it was much quieter than it had been before he'd dropped off to sleep.

Tony was sleeping peacefully next to him and everyone except one man in the corner was asleep. He was watching the television over his bed and had small headphones in his ears. He was smiling as if something he was watching was amusing him. David thought he looked much older than the rest of the men in the ward and his white wispy hair was protruding at all angles from his head. The man noticed David was looking at him and waved. David waved back and in the gentle light of the ward, David felt a connection with the old man in the corner.

Having slept for a few hours, David was now wide awake, so he shifted himself up in bed, being careful not to dislodge the wires and traces hooked up to the machines around him which continued their bleeping and flashing orchestration.

Lucy had left him the Evening Standard from that day and David picked it up to see what news had been occurring.

As he skimmed over the headlines and articles on the front page, he noticed a feeling of disconnection from the reality of the world going on around him. In just a few short hours, David had gone from eating supper with his family to sitting in hospital having had a heart attack. It was a sobering thought just how quickly life could change.

David turned over the pages of the newspaper, finding the banal headlines and news of celebrities' lives or the latest gaffe by a politician as thoroughly uninteresting. He'd just had a few of the most fascinating days of his life, when he was beginning to think differently, and yet the world seemed to have stayed the same. Lying in his bed, David realised his life had to be different now and he vowed to remember everything the magical visitors into his life had told him.

As he reached the end of his newspaper, he caught sight of an advert in the bottom right-hand corner of one of the pages. It was the picture of a man with his arm punching the air and a microphone in the other hand. The headline above the photo said, 'Be the Best' and underneath was a short description of the Robin Anton event that Lucy had mentioned. David smiled and wondered if he was being prompted to go along with Lucy. There and then he decided, as part of his new approach to life, he'd book tickets as a surprise and go with Lucy to the event in Birmingham later in the month.

His thoughts were interrupted by the gentle squeak of wheels coming down the ward. A trolley with teacups and a large steel teapot appeared around the corner, pushed by an elderly lady wearing the cream attire of a hospital orderly. On her head, she wore a small white hat which covered a small amount of unkempt white hair. She walked very slowly, shuffling along behind her trolley.

There was no sign of any nursing staff and the old lady and her tea trolley appeared to be the only person around. She walked slowly over towards David and as she got to his bedside, he noticed her name badge. Her name was Mary.

"Evenin' darlin'," she said. "Would you like a cuppa before you settle in for the night?"

"Er... yes please," said David, hoping not to wake the other men in the ward.

Mary then returned to her trolley and proceeded to make David a cup of tea. She brought it back and handed it to him.

"How's it all going then?" she asked.

"I've had a heart attack," replied David.

"Yes, I know me old china, as you're in the coronary ward. I meant, have Michael's friends been looking after you?"

David spluttered his tea and it splashed onto the crisp white bedlinen in front of him. He put the cup down on the cabinet beside his bed and took a breath.

"How do you know about Michael?" asked David.

"We all know Michael, don't we? He's only trying to help you David. Anyway, what have you learnt so far then?"

Yet again, someone who already knew his name, but this time David thought he could detect why. He caught a whiff of a smell that was pungent and decaying. It was a familiar smell.

"Have we met before? Did I meet you on my way to the park a few days ago?"

"I'm Mary and I'm too busy making tea to be walking around the park," said Mary. "Now, how are you feeling about your life now then?"

David took a sip of his tea. It was hot and sweet. "I just feel I want another chance in life. I guess I've been pushing too hard and aiming for the wrong things."

"Well, you know you've got to start to aim for less to put that right, ain't ya?"

"I know Mary. I've realised in the past few days some things about my life purpose and what's important to me."

Mary moved a little closer towards David, shuffling her feet, and David noticed an old walking stick hooked on the end of the tea trolley. The rotting smell he recognised grew stronger.

"Yes, I know about purpose David," whispered Mary. "It's the foundation for everything y'see. You were put here on this big old planet of ours to do what you're good at, are passionate about, stand for and are called to do. Sometimes, your purpose appears right in front of you without you realising, you see. Smacks you right in the head at times. Often, there is already purpose in your life, but you just need to step back and take some time to really understand it all. Many people only do this when they end up in a place like this. But you don't need to wait until you've had a heart attack, lost someone you love or experienced a life crisis. Remember, you just need to go into the silence and start to think about it. Find the church in your mind where you can go to and talk to the silence. It's there you'll get the most important answers to your deepest questions, me old china."

Mary touched David's hand and for a moment the lights above his head flickered and buzzed. She shuffled back to the trolley and turned it around. As she walked back along the ward and the squeaking faded into the distance, Jane, who was one of the nurses on night duty, appeared and began picking up the clipboards on the end of the beds. She was one of the older and more experienced nurses, short, with long black hair tied in a ponytail. She got to David's bed and he was sitting up drinking the remainder of his tea.

"Where did you get the tea from David?" she asked.

"Mary just brought it round," he replied.

"Who's Mary?" asked Jane as she picked up the clipboard from the end of his bed.

"You know, Mary with the tea trolley. She's just come round and offered us tea."

Jane looked at David. "There's no-one called Mary who works on this ward and we don't have tea trolleys at 11.30pm David. I think you're telling me porky pies." Seemingly unperturbed by the appearance of David's teacup, she took it from David and put it back onto the cabinet by his bed. Then she started to plump up the pillows behind David's head and tucked in his sheets. "It's important you get some rest now David as you're going home tomorrow."

Within a few moments she'd moved on to another bed.

David looked across at the old man who'd been watching television. The old man winked at him and smiled.

David lay back down on his bed and thought about Mary and what she'd said about finding his purpose. As he drifted off to sleep, he caught sight of the old man opposite, who was now cleaning his glasses with a crisp white hand-kerchief. The old man smiled, and David drifted off into a peaceful sleep.

He woke with a start and for a moment, he couldn't recall where he was.

Slowly, his mind cleared and along with the bleeps and flashes from the machines on the ward, he remembered he'd had a heart attack. He also remembered his visit from the curious tea lady called Mary and how she'd told him to go into the silence to find who he was.

The clock on the wall said 4.11am and it was still dark outside. The ward was silent, the old man opposite was fast asleep, and David decided to listen to see if the silence that Michael had told him about could tell him something.

He remembered the advert in the paper he'd seen about the 'Be the Best' conference and he wondered if he should insist on going along with Lucy. He asked himself the question in his mind.

"Yes," was the reply in his head.

David looked around to see where the voice had come from but everyone else in the ward was sleeping and there was no sign of a nurse or other members of staff.

David asked about the event again in his mind and again, the answer came back and was immediate. He recognised the voice. It was his own voice inside his head, and he was simply talking to himself. He decided to play along with the game and see if he could answer any more of his own questions.

"Am I going to come through this tough period?" he asked the silence in his head.

"Yes," came the reply.

"Am I going to die soon?" he asked the silence again.

"No," came the reply.

"Am I a good man?" David asked, enjoying the game.

"Yes, you are. Not perfect, but you're a good man."

David smiled. He enjoyed talking to the silence.

"I'm more than the silence," responded the voice inside his head.

David was puzzled. He hadn't asked the silence a question, but it had responded anyway. He looked around again. His voice sounded so clear in his head. It was if the voice was around him and inside of him. It was his own voice and yet it 'felt' different.

He could feel his eyes getting heavy and he wanted to sleep.

"I'm going to rest now," he thought inside his head.

"Be at rest. Then you can be the best."

David knew being the best was something he'd craved for a long time, and as he drifted off to sleep, he thought again about the 'Be the Best' conference. Maybe the silence wanted him to go along.

He closed his eyes and drifted back to sleep.

10.

David was woken up at 6.30am for observations, and a new nurse was on duty. Her name was Claire and her shoulder length blonde hair was pulled back into a ponytail emerging from the top of her head. She was short and slim with no make-up at all and yet her freshness and cheerful demeanour was a genuine boost to David's mood.

She took his temperature by placing a modern electronic thermometer and checked his blood pressure.

"She's a bit of alright ain't she, me old china?"

It was Tony who was now awake and waiting for Claire to come around to his bed and do his observations.

"Hello gorgeous," he said, and Claire looked up from one of the charts she was studying.

"Morning Tony. Did you sleep well?"

"Like a baby," replied Tony. "Better not take me temperature though darlin'. With ya around, it's bound to be rising. And not just me temperature either!"

Claire blushed and David felt uncomfortable with Tony's flirtatious remarks. He was clearly embarrassing her, but he didn't seem to care. He was revelling in her discomfort.

"What I'd really like is a bed bath though darlin'. Any chance of giving an old man a bit of a freshen up this morning, if ya know what I mean?" Tony winked at Claire and she simply blushed even more.

"The only thing you'll be getting from me is a slap if you continue with your chatter Tony. Settle down and let me do my work." She placed the folder with his charts in back in the holder on the end of the bed and walked away towards the main nurses' station.

Tony watched her walk away and David cringed, wondering what thoughts were going through his mind.

"Lust might be one of the deadly sins me old china, but cor blimey, she's a stunner that one ain't she?"

David wasn't sure what to say. Tony's lecherous approaches had made him feel very uncomfortable. It was just not right.

"I guess with daughters of my own about the same age, it just doesn't feel right to be lusting over someone who's just trying to do her job."

"Nah, come off it me old china. You'd do her just as much as the next bloke."

"No Tony. I wouldn't."

David wanted the conversation to end and whilst he had enjoyed Tony's company at first, now he wished he was in a different ward. This clash of perspectives had changed his view completely and he no longer wanted to listen to his cockney slang or perverted views.

"I'm only playin' about mate. No need to take offence as none is intended." Tony smiled at David and winked again.

"OK Tony, but I just think we need to show some respect to Claire. She is looking after us, isn't she?"

Tony looked a little sheepish and embarrassed. "Yeah, I sometimes let my mouth engage before me watch and chain. It's a curse at times. Sorry if I offended ya mate."

David relaxed a little more and changed the subject. For a few minutes they discussed Arsenal and West Ham and the merits of both football teams, their stadiums and their owners. Tony was an East End boy who had watched West

Ham play since he was small. The conversation flowed and they laughed together and enjoyed the banter.

David had found some common ground with Tony and it felt much more comfortable. By the time Claire returned to the ward to conduct more observations, the previous uncomfortable atmosphere had been replaced with jovial and pleasant chatter.

Just as Claire was about to leave the ward again, Tony called her over to his bed. David cringed, thinking Tony was about to start flirting with the young girl again.

He touched her arm and looked up at her. "Just wanted to apologise for being a Michael Caine earlier. Can't help meself sometimes, but if I offended ya love, I need to apologise. No offence meant me old china."

David thought Claire looked relieved as she placed Tony's hand back on the bed. "I've heard a lot worse Tony, so you just focus on resting and getting better. Then we can all be happy eh?"

It was Tony's turn to blush, but David admired his willingness to apologise. Tony wasn't a bad person, but he just didn't seem to think the way David did. Maybe it was just a clash of perspectives or personal values, but David decided to let it lie for now.

When Lucy arrived later in the morning, David was already dressed and ready to be discharged. He was sitting in the chair next to the bed, reading a newspaper.

"Morning love, have they said you can come home then?" She put her hands on the arms of his chair and kissed his forehead. She sat down on the bed.

"You'd best grab a chair Lucy as they don't like you sitting on the bed."

"Since when have you followed the rules?" said Lucy, getting up from the bed and heading over towards a stack of chairs piled up against a wall. She returned with a tired and rather tatty plastic chair and sat in front of David.

"Are Langham's OK with you taking the time off today?"

"Yes of course. I called in on the way here and told James what had happened. He was genuinely concerned for you and told me to take the rest of the day off. After all the years I've been there, I deserve some compassionate leave he said. I then came straight here. Did you sleep OK?"

"Not too bad, I guess. I was awake around 4am but the ward was very quiet, so I was able to spend some time thinking."

"Oh yes? What were you thinking about then?"

"I want us to go to the 'Be the Best' conference together."

"You do? What's with the change of heart?"

They both laughed.

"Maybe that's exactly it," said David. "Maybe it's created a change of heart within me too."

Lucy laughed. "A change of heart? That's funny David, when you're sitting there recovering from a heart attack!"

David picked up Lucy's left hand. "Listen love, we've been married a long time and been through a lot together. When we lost Peter, I thought we'd never be able to survive, but we did. This is just another setback and one we'll get through. But I want things to be different and maybe if we go to the conference together, I'll hear something or meet someone and then I'll see the light and know what you've been talking about these last few months."

"But I don't want you to go just because you think you should. If you're going to come with me, then I want it to be because you want to for yourself. This heart attack is a warning David that something must change. But you must want to change."

"I know," said David. "There are parts of me I don't want to change though too." He leaned forward and lowered his voice. "Tony was flirting with the young nurse over there and

I got really uncomfortable. It made me feel sick. He's apologised to her now but that's something I wouldn't want to change about me. My core values are still important to me."

Lucy picked up David's other hand and held them both. She looked directly into his eyes and spoke softly. "It's why I love you David. Your values are something you've stood by and it's what drives you. I admire you for this, and all that happened was your values clashed with his. It happens. Don't be angry with him as he's a good old sort really."

David hadn't considered that Tony's flirting with Claire could be a clash of values, but he thought Lucy was right.

"Good morning Mr Turner, how are you this morning?"

It was Dr. Patel and Lucy stood up quickly to let him come alongside David, who smiled at her sudden flustering.

"Morning doctor, I'm feeling really good actually. Keen to get home as soon as I can if you'll let me go of course!"

Dr. Patel was looking through the notes in the folder at the end of David's bed and he appeared to scribble a few notes.

"Well, your observations have been stable overnight, and the tests yesterday confirmed what we knew, so it's about lifestyle changes now Mr Turner. Have you seen the cardiac rehabilitation team yet?"

"No doc. Not yet."

"Well you can't be discharged until you've seen one of the team. But I'll put in your notes that you can go once they've seen you, OK?"

"That's great doc, thank you."

"Don't thank me, thank your guardian angels Mr Turner. You had a lucky escape this time, but next time the ending may be very different if you don't look after your health."

He placed the folder back in its holder and moved across the ward to another patient.

David sat back in his chair, considering what Dr Patel had said. He knew he needed to take his health more seriously and that the heart attack had certainly been a wake-up call. Maybe it was time to place his health as a higher priority. After all, if he was to save the business, he'd need to be around to enjoy the fruits of his labours.

"Let's go to the conference together Lucy," he said. "I want to change things in my life and not just in the business either. The last few days have shown me so much about my life that needs to change. To be honest, it's hard to know where to start. I've met many people who've shown me life can be different. But I'm still unsure what I need to do."

Lucy looked puzzled. "You sound like our life is awful David, but I don't think it is."

David reached out and took Lucy's hand once more. "Our life is amazing love, but I think I'm being guided in some way to review how I've looked at my own life. It's as if I've been sent a set of messengers to give me different perspectives. And it's made me think about my values and how authentic and real I'm being."

"Robin Anton talks about being authentic all the time David. Maybe we should go to the conference after all."

"Mr Turner? I'm sorry to interrupt you both but I'm Alison Smith, one of the cardiac rehabilitation team here and Dr Patel has asked me to see you before you go."

Alison Smith was short and slightly overweight, so her pale blue uniform tugged and fought with her frame as she moved around. With very short hair and rugged jaw, David immediately thought she had a masculine air about her.

Alison picked up David's notes from the end of the bed and quickly skimmed through them. "I see you've had a lucky escape then. Just a warning sign for now. Looks like someone up there is looking out for you. Many men of your age don't come back from a scare like this. How much exercise do you do now David?"

Her brusque manner was doing nothing to allay David's thoughts about her masculine demeanour. "I do walk every morning around Highgate Park but nothing other than that," he said.

"Well, a little exercise every day is all we recommend. Many people who come in here with a scare suddenly think they must make wholesale changes to their lives and start signing up for marathons and join gyms. All we want people to do is change their lifestyle a little. Do you drink much David?"

David visualised the collection of wine bottles left out each week for the council refuse department, but he wasn't about to admit to his scary new friend just how many bottles were consumed on a weekly basis.

"Er, a little I guess," said David.

"How many glasses?" said Alison.

Glasses? More like bottles, thought David. "About six glasses a week."

"Liar," said Lucy. "You know you've been drinking more and more recently and despite me telling you how much sugar is in a glass of wine, you know you drink three or four bottles a week. There's no point in pretending David."

"I'm not an alcoholic though, am I? I don't *need* a drink. I just like a glass of wine at the end of the day to help me unwind."

"Ah yes, Mr Turner, but your few glasses a week to help you unwind has wound you up in here." Alison was grinning with her clever pun. "You need to cut down on the wine and improve your exercise programme." She reached into a pocket on the side of her tunic and pulled out a folded piece of paper. She unfolded it and handed it to David.

"On this sheet are a few exercises for you to do when you're at home, some diet advice and some ideas for how far you need to be walking every day. Then hopefully, we won't see you again. Take care of yourself, and if you need to chat to any of us, our number is on the bottom of the sheet. Take care." Alison was off and out of the ward before David had a chance to ask any questions at all.

David looked at Lucy and waved the piece of paper in her direction. "So, this is my advice. One scrappy piece of paper from a lady who seemed uninterested in her job and didn't seem to care about what happened to me or of the stress resulting in my heart attack. A lot of bloody use she was."

"Stop it David. She was just doing her job and it must be a thankless task, as I bet many people ignore the advice she gives them. She must get demoralised with all the people who come through the doors of the hospital with conditions which are entirely avoidable if we would just take the good advice available to us. Anyway, you're a fine one to talk. We've been telling you for ages to slow down or you'll get a heart attack. You wouldn't be walking around the park in the morning if I hadn't encouraged you to do it. You always seem to ignore advice, even when you know it's right."

David thought about all the advice he'd been given by the people he'd met over the last few days. He didn't want to ignore it anymore. He knew he had to change his life and step into a different future.

"I don't want to ignore advice anymore Lucy, even it is from ladies in tight-fitting uniforms. I do want to change, which is why I'm suggesting we go to the 'Be the Best' conference together."

Lucy reached out and touched David's hand. "OK love, we'll go together. I can't tell you to take advice and then stop you from going to a conference full of advice, can I?"

Lucy and David laughed, and he realised just how much he loved this woman who'd been at his side through so many of his most difficult challenges.

"I love you," he said.

"You too," she replied.

"Your taxi's here," said Jane, who was still on duty, despite being on the ward during the night. David wondered how some of the nursing staff managed to survive when they worked such long shifts.

"Thanks Jane. I'm surprised you're still here. What time do you finish?" David asked.

"Nearly done now. Just got your discharge forms to do and then I can go home."

"How do you do it Jane?" asked David, still curious to know why nurses were so dedicated.

"Well, it's not easy and sometimes I do wonder why I've been in nursing so long. But it's my calling, I guess. I could never imagine doing something else and when I'm working the time just seems to fly by, even in the quiet and dark of the middle of the night. Anyway, you need to be making sure you don't come back in here soon David. Are you going to look after yourself?"

"He will," said Lucy who had been listening intently to what Jane had been saying. "I'll make sure he takes care of himself."

David stood up slowly and Lucy took his arm. "Let's just take it steady, you can lean on me."

"I've leant on you for a long time love. It's time I stood on my own two feet in more ways than one."

"That's fighting talk," said Jane. "Good on you David. You'll need these forms. The top one needs to go to your GP, so he knows you've been in here. You take care of yourself and let's NOT see you soon." Jane smiled at him and headed back towards the nurses' station.

David watched Jane stride back to colleagues with energy and purpose, even after a long nightshift. He yearned to have her passion and enthusiasm. And maybe her calling too. He realised Jane was probably using her purpose to sustain her.

"Come on Lucy, let's get out of here. I need some air."

"Are ya leavin' us then me old china?"

"Yes Tony, I've been allowed out on good behaviour!"

"Well, you're buggered then ain't ya? None of us know how to have good behaviour do we?" he laughed, and Lucy and David laughed with him. "You take care of the trouble and strife too – she's a good'un that one I can tell ya."

"I will Tony. It's been a pleasure to meet you and spend some time in your company. I hope you get out soon."

"I should be out tomorrow they reckon. Just got a few more tests to run on me ticker before they let me back to the rat race. You take care now and thanks for helping me see where I was going wrong before, ya know, with *that* situation…" Tony winked and nodded his head towards the nurses' station where Claire was working.

"It's fine Tony, you helped me see some things too. Maybe that's what this was about; us both learning some-thing from each other to take forward into our lives, so we change them for the better."

"Blimey, I'm not even sure I know what you're talking about David, but I've enjoyed meeting ya, so stay safe mate."

David shook Tony's hand warmly and then put his arm through Lucy's so he could walk with her. Lucy had brought some clean clothes from home which David had changed into and she was carrying the rest of his things in a small plastic bag.

"Bye Tony. You be good now!" said Lucy.

"I'll do me best me old china!"

As they walked slowly towards the exit of the ward, David noticed just how many men were wired up to machines, sleeping quietly or sitting up in bed reading or watching their televisions. The ward was full of men; some older and some younger than him, but all with the same problem – a heart almost broken under the strain of life.

David could feel a well of emotion coming up inside him for all the men who pushed themselves hard to succeed and ended up in coronary wards all over the country and the world. His mind visualised rows and rows of men and women who nearly killed themselves striving for some sort of success which eluded them in the same way it had for David.

"I can't come back here Lucy. Something has to change within me."

"I think it already has David." She squeezed his hand and looked up at him. "For the first time since we lost Peter, I really think you do want to change."

They walked the remaining distance through the long corridors to the exit of the hospital. Just outside the exit the taxi was waiting. As they walked towards the taxi, which David recognised as an old Mercedes C Class, the driver got out of the car and came round to open the doors for them.

"Good morning sir. Let me help you. And you madam. My name is Abdul and I'm here to take you home. Can I please have your names?"

"Hello Abdul, we're David and Lucy Turner," said David. "Nice to meet you Abdul."

David was struck by the greeting from the taxi driver. Usually, you'd be expected to open your own door and climb in unaided whilst the driver waited, often impatiently, for you to get in his taxi. But Abdul was fussing around them as if they were royalty. He shut the doors on both sides of the car and got back into the driving seat.

Inside the taxi, David noticed the spotless and fresh interior. The aging leather seats shone as if they been polished and the carpets were without any marks or dirt. Hanging from the rear-view mirror was a triangular pennant made up of three colours which David recognised as being from Afghanistan.

Abdul looked back at David through the rear-view mirror. "Please put your seatbelts on. They are both in full working order and I'd like you to be safe, so please, put on your seatbelts."

David and Lucy both duly obliged and smiled at each other at Abdul's insistence and concerned manner.

"Where am I taking you to please? May I have the address including postcode please?"

David and Lucy exchanged glances again and Lucy answered. "Number 32, Hillway, Highgate, N6 6DP. It's not far."

"Ah yes, I know Hillway," said Abdul. "Just the other side of the park. Very nice. I not need my sat nav as I know this road. Please sit back and enjoy the ride in my taxi."

David was curious about Abdul. He seemed very proud of his taxi and David wondered how long he'd been in the country, as his accent was still very strong, even though his use of English was very clear.

"How long have you had your taxi Abdul? It's a very smart car, particularly for its age."

"I've been here since two years. I come from Afghanistan. Very bad country. I make it with my family to England where people very nice. We had long journey to come here. Very dangerous. But I want to work to look after my family. I wash cars for one year. Very hard work for very poor money but we save hard. And owner of car wash has taxi firm too, so he let me use this taxi to make more money for my family."

David and Lucy were both now leaning forwards and in the middle of the back seat, curious to know more about their dedicated taxi driver.

Lucy spoke first. "Why did you leave Afghanistan, Abdul, and how did you get here?"

"My country very bad. Too many people dying and being killed. My family in danger. I have young daughter Hadiya.

She was a gift from God to us. Our country too dangerous for her so we walk to border and leave country. We travel for 3 months on train, buses and boats. We get to England and come to London and I start working in car wash."

David and Lucy were gripped by Abdul's story, and as he drove them through the busy London streets, Abdul explained more about the perils of their journey across Europe to the UK and how they had to fight to be granted asylum. They were now living in a small flat in Ealing and his daughter had started school.

David was moved by Abdul's dedication to provide for his family and give them a better life. But he was different to many he'd met in the UK, who saw bigger houses and cars as providing a better life. "Why did you try so hard to come here Abdul?"

"England is a good country with good people. We know we'd be helped here. You are kind. I want my daughter to have chance for life I not had. Sabiha and me just want best for Hadiya."

"How is your life now?" asked Lucy.

"I am wealthy man now. I have flat and job. We have food to eat and my daughter goes to school. In my country, this makes me a wealthy man. God has blessed me and my family."

David was moved by this man's dedication to his family and the pride in which it showed in his own life. "You are clearly a proud man Abdul. You're an example to many others, including me." David squeezed Lucy's hand.

"You come from hospital. Have you been sick?" asked Abdul.

"I had a heart attack, but I've been given a second chance now, so I've got to take it."

The taxi swung around into Hillway and headed up towards their house, but David didn't want the journey to end. He was enjoying listening to Abdul. "Do you miss your home country Abdul?"

"I miss my brothers, who are now with God, and I miss some of my friends. But I've made new friends, and this is my home now. I am blessed and lucky to be alive and living in great country. I drive lovely taxi and meet lovely people like you Mr David."

Abdul pulled the taxi up in front of number 32. "Is this your house? Lovely house. You very lucky to live in nice house like this in London. One day, I will have house like this for my family."

David didn't doubt Abdul would reach his dream. "You keep working hard Abdul and you'll reach you dreams. One day, you could live in a house like ours, I'm certain of it."

Abdul turned around and looked straight at David. "Your house very nice but I already reach my dream. I have safe place to live now. My daughter go to school and learn English. My wife safe at night. I may have less but I have much more than the beggars on the street or those who sleep in the graveyard over there. I am lucky man. I thank God every day for him bringing me here. This is why I have already reached my dream."

Lucy handed Abdul a £20 note for the £8 fare. "Keep the change Abdul. It's been a pleasure to spend time in your taxi."

"Oh no, too much tip. I just do my job." He reached into a small purse and handed a £10 note back to Lucy. David took the note from Lucy.

"Abdul. Please put out your hand."

Abdul reached back towards David and David folded up the £10 note and placed it into his open palm. "Take this and buy something for Sabiha. Maybe take her some flowers. You've inspired me this morning and this is the only way I can show you how much. Will you take it please?"

Abdul was shaking his head. "People in this country think happiness is through money. I very grateful and thank you for your money and yes, I will buy flowers for Sabiha. She loves flowers. But please, Mr David. If you remember Abdul in your prayers please. And please look at your life and know how God has blessed you. You too Miss Lucy."

"We will Abdul," said Lucy. "Thanks for bringing us home in your lovely taxi."

Lucy climbed out of the car and came round to help David.

As David went to climb out of the car, he stopped and placed his hand on the shoulder of Abdul. "You're an inspiration to me. You've had little in your life and yet you're far wealthier than me. You've made my heart sing this morning and I hope to see you again."

"You're welcome Mr David. Have a good day. If you ever need taxi, please call this number." Abdul passed a small business card to David which simply had his name and a telephone number on it.

"I will Abdul, God bless you."

David climbed out of the car and Lucy supported him as they walked slowly up the path towards their front door. David looked back to wave to Abdul, but the car was already moving off. Within a few seconds, Abdul had disappeared around the corner and the Mercedes was out of sight.

"What an amazing man," said Lucy. "To think he risked his life and his family, just to get here. Many in this country moan and complain about how little they have or how awful things are. And yet, he's grateful for such small things."

"I guess he understands the concept of aiming for less," said David. "He's found happiness and contentment by simply believing what he already has is enough. He doesn't need our big house to be happy. Gosh, it's a sobering thought isn't it?"

They arrived at the front door and Lucy reached into her handbag to find her keys. She took them and placed a key in the lock and opened the door. "Come on then Mr David. It's time for you to start a new life."

David smiled. He knew his new life had already started.

As he stepped back into his house, he thought of Abdul and asked God to take care of him.

A voice inside his head replied. "It is done."

David still had the business card in his hand. He looked down at it and noticed there were words on both sides of the card. On the reverse side to Abdul's name and number was a quote. It said, *'So lose not heart, or fall into despair, for you will be superior if you are true in faith' Surat Al-i'iram [3:139]*. David didn't recognise the quote but assumed it was from the Quran. But what he did recognise was the message. He knew that Abdul's story was one of faith against all the odds. He knew he must have faith and that his life could be different if he simply chose it to be so.

PART
TWO

11.

When the alarm went off, David regretted the champagne of the previous evening. Annabel had decided they should all celebrate the fact her dad had last week survived his heart attack, and they spent the evening talking, chatting and planning an exciting future together. Even Georgia was upbeat and talked of changing her job and being more positive.

But there was nothing positive about David's headache, which was simply self-induced. He pulled back the covers to get out of bed and could feel the tenderness across his chest where the ambulance crew, followed by the hospital staff, had thumped his chest and stuck wires all over him.

Lucy was still sleeping, as the alarm hadn't disturbed her. She rarely drank alcohol but had been caught up in the excitement and had drunk a few more glasses of champagne than her body could cope with.

David watched her body rise and fall with each breath, a silent sign she was alive. Her slim body was a testament to how well she took care of herself. From a sensible diet to regular trips to the gym, she kept herself fit and had clearly been an inspiration to Annabel and Georgia. She was an inspiration to him too and he wondered just how close he had come to his last breath, and his resolve to change his approach to life returned.

Creeping across the bedroom, trying to avoid the familiar squeaky floorboards, he pulled on his jogging trousers and t-shirt. He picked up his running shoes that even in his semi-drunkenness before bed, he'd remembered to place where he could find them in the dark and opened the bedroom door. Tiptoeing down the landing, he headed downstairs.

Through the early morning light, he spotted something sticking through the letterbox. As he reached the bottom of the stairs, he could see another red envelope poking through. With his running shoes still in his hand, he pulled the envelope from the letterbox and sat down on the stairs behind him.

The letter was addressed to 'The New David'. There were no other details and there was no stamp or franking on the envelope, so it must have been delivered by hand.

David opened the envelope, which was empty. He turned it back over again and wondered why someone would send him another empty red envelope. He looked back inside the envelope and in the dim light of the hallway, he noticed a few words written on the inside of the envelope. *'The envelope is empty. It's time to choose what to place in it.'*

David stared at the words, grasping for meaning. Why would someone place another envelope through his letterbox? Was someone playing games with him? He placed the envelope on the stair next to him and began to put on his running shoes. He then picked up the envelope again and folded it in two, placing it in the pocket of his jogging trousers. Stepping towards the front door he stopped and took the envelope out of his pocket and read the text once more. He wondered if it was a message about his life.

He placed the envelope back into his pocket and opened the front door. The sun was just rising, and the light was barely breaking through the clouds above but as he took his first few steps away from the house, the world felt different, as if the colours all around him had changed. He felt lightheaded and stopped along the path. He took a deep breath and headed away from the house and down his street towards the park.

As he arrived at the usual gate, the robin was there to greet him. It chirped busily and kept moving it's head, as if it was noticing something different about David too. David smiled.

"You can see it too, can't you? There's something different about the world today isn't there?"

The robin chirped back in agreement and David stepped into the park. The warmth of the rising sun was creating an eerie mist along the ground, forming an unearthly atmosphere. David couldn't see anyone else, so he decided to gently jog along his usual route rather than walk, as he knew he had to take on board the cardiac team's advice. It was the first time since hospital that he'd attempted more than a slow walk.

He headed towards the cemetery at the back of the park and as he ran slowly along paths bordered by the morning mist, he felt invigorated and alive.

As he turned a corner in-between two hedges, he was startled by a man sweeping the footpaths. David skidded to a halt and began to walk slowly past the man who continued to broom the footpath. He was tall and wearing grey overalls with black hobnailed boots on his feet, scraping the ground as he moved. He wore a matching grey cap on his head from which long hair protruded down over his shoulders. As David reached him, he turned his head and David could see he had a moustache and was unshaven. He looked very dishevelled and unkempt.

"Morning," said David politely.

"Aye, it be that," he said in a strong Scottish accent that David thought was more Glaswegian than Edinburgh.

David continued to walk past the man, who continued to broom.

"You see, it's all in the leaves and the mist," said the man.

David stopped walking. "Sorry?"

"It's all in the leaves and the mist. Don't you see it?" He was now standing up and leaning with both hands crossed on the top of the broom handle. "The old leaves fall away and as the mist rises in the morning, the new leaves appear sure enough."

David started to walk away from the strange path sweeper.

"Ah... but do ye really see it? I can sweep away the old but ye have to make way for the new don't ye laddie? And don't let the mist of the new morning fool ye. The new leaves are there if ye look deeply enough."

David wondered if this man could be another of the strange encounters shaping his life over the last few weeks, or if he was just imagining something which was pure coincidence.

"There's no such thing as chance laddie. Every pathway is laid out ahead of ye, ye just need to keep walking." The man pointed away towards the back of the park. "If ye keep walking, eventually the mist will clear, and ye see what's new. But ye have to keep walking."

The man put his hand in his pocket and pulled out a red handkerchief and wiped his brow. "It sure is hard work keeping these pathways clear." He placed his handkerchief back in his pocket and winked at David.

David shivered. A strong sense of déjà vu came over him.

"Er, thanks. I'd best be going now. So, I'll see you." David turned and started to walk away from the man, who felt strangely familiar.

"Not unless I see ye first!" shouted the man.

David didn't look back and gently broke into a jog. Soon he'd left the strange path-sweeper behind. As he jogged, he allowed his mind to wander, and asked the silence who the man was and if he was important.

"Everyone's important," came back the reply.

He wondered if the man had told him something important that he was meant to remember.

"Everything's important," said the silence.

As David arrived back at the exit of the park, the robin was still waiting for him. "Are you important?" he asked the robin. The robin gave him two quick chirps and David felt it was saying, "Of course!"

David walked back towards the house, still thinking about the path-sweeper in the park. As he walked up the path to his house, he remembered the red envelope in his pocket, and he reached in and pulled it out once more.

As he unfolded the envelope something fell out of the envelope. David picked it up. It was a bright green leaf, fresh and damp, covered in a layer of morning mist. Inside the envelope some words were still there, but David was certain the words were now different. The words read, *'The envelope was empty. You chose a fresh start.'*

David smiled and placed the new leaf back into the folded envelope. He put the envelope back in his pocket, recognising that the magical encounters were continuing, and he was excited to see where his life was going next.

As he entered the front door, the smell of fresh toast and coffee greeted him in a sensory rush. He sat down on the stairs and removed his running shoes, placing them under the stairs. He entered the kitchen and Lucy was sitting at the same table where only a few days before, David had endured a heart attack. She was reading a magazine.

"Morning love," said David.

Lucy looked up. "Oh hiya – how was your walk this morning?"

"Well, it was a gentle run actually. Got to start afresh with a new approach Lucy, so I jogged this morning."

Lucy frowned. "Are you sure you should be running – you had a heart attack only a few days ago."

"It's fine, you worry too much. I enjoyed it, there was a mist across the grass, and everything smelt fresh and alive. I felt alive too Lucy."

"Well you're lucky to be so, I'm glad you recognise that!" Lucy looked back at her magazine. "Did you meet any strange people this morning?"

David thought about the path-sweeper and the fresh new leaf in the red envelope which had appeared in the letterbox. "No, nothing unusual this morning love. What are you reading?"

Lucy put down the magazine. "I was just looking at an advert for that 'Be the Best' conference. Do you still want to go or was it just something you said in the hospital to reassure me?"

David came around the table and put his arm round Lucy's shoulders. "Today I turn over a new leaf Lucy. I don't want to be sceptical and doubtful all the time. I want us to go to this together and I want you to show me a book to read to help me too."

"Crikey. I think I'll let you have a heart attack more often if it's going to get you to move your opinion this much."

David kissed Lucy on the cheek. "Maybe my heart attack was a wake-up call Lucy. Maybe I should move in a different direction, which has to start with my attitudes and beliefs doesn't it?" He sat down opposite Lucy.

"Let's have a look at the advert then."

Lucy pushed the magazine across the table towards him and David turned it round to face him. The advert showed a man on a stage in front of a large screen. He had his hands in the air, a headset microphone around his face and he was clearly shouting something to a huge audience of people in front of him, who all had their hands in the air too. The headline at the top of the advert was 'Do you want to be the best?'

David screwed up his face involuntarily at the thought of being in an audience of over-excited, highly-charged and falsely-positive people. Lucy spotted the change in his face.

"You don't really want to go do you?" she said.

David didn't want to lie and pretend he felt comfortable about being amongst people who seemed to worship this charismatic speaker. But he did want to change and could see from the looks on the faces of those in the audience in the picture, they were feeling something positive, even if it was a falsely produced emotion.

"It's not that I don't want to go Lucy, it's just I find all this hero-worshipping of these speakers a little unnerving. Surely, we need to work out ourselves how to be more positive or how to get our lives in order. Why do we need these speakers, who are no doubt earning fortunes, playing on the emotions of those who are just seeking to feel better about themselves, their lives or maybe even their work?"

Lucy took the magazine back from David. "If you read the blurb underneath rather than being quick to judge, you'd have seen many of the speakers are people like you who've been through a difficult time in their lives, have come through it and want to share it with others to help them. What's wrong with that?"

"There's nothing wrong with it particularly, but why do they feel they need to get up on stage, charge people a fortune to listen and promise them things they can't guarantee at all."

Lucy closed the magazine and got up from the table and started to fill the kettle to make some tea. "Nothing can be done to change a closed mind David. You say you want to change but you dismiss those who've changed their lives for the better and assume there's nothing you can take from their experience. Surely, when we've been through tough times, one of the best things we can do is to help others with our wisdom and experience?"

"Yes Lucy, I get it, I really do, and my mind is open. The last couple of weeks have shown me I must have an open mind or else I wouldn't be able to learn what I've been learning about life. Let's book a couple of tickets and make a weekend of it. We can stay in a nice hotel and get away for a couple of nights and surround ourselves with positive people. That can't be a bad thing can it?"

Lucy had been washing up some dishes with her back to David and she turned to face him, pointing her finger contained within a bright yellow, rubber glove. "That, my dear wonderful husband, is the most sensible thing you've said in a long time."

David winked at her. "It's amazing what a heart attack and a few strange encounters can do to change your perspective isn't it?"

The kettle boiled and David got up to make a pot of tea.

Over the next hour, David and Lucy opened David's laptop and found the website for the 'Be the Best' conference being held near Birmingham. They booked their tickets for the event, but as it was just two weeks away, they struggled to find a hotel to accommodate them, as the hotel nearest to the conference centre was already full. They did find a hotel about half a mile from the venue, which meant they could walk without having to get a taxi. They also booked train tickets to get them from London to Birmingham. The conference was over a weekend, so they planned to arrive on the Friday night and leave on the Sunday afternoon.

By the time everything was booked, they realised they were in danger of being late for work. Lucy showered first and David followed quickly afterwards. They both dashed out of the house and headed off for work, and in David's case, just one week after having a heart attack.

12.

As David drove towards the depot where he'd spent years trying to build a successful business, he felt different. It didn't matter so much to him whether the business succeeded or failed. He'd just spent an exciting hour with Lucy planning a different future and he wasn't sure if this business would still be part of it. He remembered the path-sweeper and his comment about knowing new life was beginning even when it was hidden from view, and he felt invigorated. A new life was certainly beginning, and he was determined to live it fully.

He pulled into the car park behind the depot and was immediately greeted by Eric who saluted as he drove into his allocated space. Eric opened the door for him.

"Mornin' guvnor. I didn't think you'd be in work today so soon after your heart attack. Are you sure you should be working?"

David climbed out of the car and handed Eric the keys. "I'm fine Eric – really good in fact. It's been a bit of a wake-up call, but the docs told me to keep active and change my life-style, so that's what I'm intending to do."

'Well, you just take it easy, you hear. Life ain't easy but you sure don't need to make it harder for yerself by working too hard."

"Bless you Eric. I promise I'll slow down a little."

'You just be sure you do guvnor, as we need you to lead us. Oh, and pay our wages!"

Eric laughed and David laughed with him as he walked across the car park to the back door of the depot. A delivery was being unloaded into the warehouse and a forklift truck was carefully unloading a pallet from the back of a truck backed up against the roller shutter door of the warehouse.

David entered the depot and began to walk towards his office.

"Morning David! What are you doing here?" said Melissa, walking towards him. "You're supposed to be at home resting."

"There's no peace for the wicked Melissa," said David, grinning like a cat that had got the cream.

"Well, it's lovely to have you back. I'll pop into your office in a few minutes and give you an update on a few things that have happened whilst you've been away. It might only have been a few days, but you won't believe what's been happening!"

Melissa was surprisingly upbeat for someone who was usually pragmatic and at times, cynical. Her positive demeanour seemed to reflect how he was feeling about life.

"Morning Billy!" called David across the depot to Billy, who was busy behind the trade counter.

"Morning Mr Turner. Great to see you. Has Melissa told you about K. Bailey and Sons?"

"No, she hasn't yet Billy, but I'll let her explain. See you later."

David walked towards his office, wondering about what had happened with K. Bailey and Sons. They were a very large engineering business working on some large construction projects in London, including the new tube line being built across the city. David had approached them several times to become a supplier but was pushed back every time for being 'too small'.

He entered his office and stopped. The office was spotlessly clean and all the papers from his desk had gone. He wondered if he'd stepped into the right office.

"What do you think then?" said Melissa from behind him. She was standing with a hot cup of tea in her hand, smiling at David. "I figured your office might've been part of your stress David, so I decided to tidy it up for you. I hope that's OK?" She walked around his desk and placed the cup of tea on the desk.

"No paper cups then Mel?" was all David could think of to say.

"No David. I decided we needed to think and behave differently from now on if we are going to be the best we can be."

David smiled.

"And having tea in proper china cups is a start David. I think it's time we began to think of ourselves as the best in the industry."

"Gosh Mel, you sound like Lucy. Have you been talking to her or reading one of her books?"

"No David, but I've been listening to some old audio CDs I found in your desk. There was one by someone called Robin Anton and it was obviously from a live event. It was a bit 'American' for me but much of what he said made sense. I realised it was time I stepped forward in my life and did more of what I love to do so I began by getting your office organised. I found loads of old papers which I've placed in the archive cupboard and I've created a new filing system for your filing cabinet."

She walked over to the large filing cabinet behind the desk and pulled open the top drawer.

"As you can see, all the slots now have tabs on them with customer names or subject matters, so you'll be able to find things much more easily. No more rummaging through piles of papers to find the things you're looking for."

David stood watching Melissa move around the office and there was something very different about her manner. He noticed too, her hair was styled slightly differently, and she was wearing a scarf around her neck, something she had never done before.

"Crikey Mel, what's come over you? This is fabulous and I'm really grateful."

David walked around the desk and sat down. Everything about the office was different, not only in the way that Mel had tidied up but there was also something else. Something less obvious but no less tangible. Whilst he was aware of some changes in thoughts before he'd had his heart attack, now it was action that was changing. Melissa had done something to make things different, rather than just thinking about it. There was a new energy, both in the office and the depot. It all seemed to stem from Melissa herself.

"Sit down Mel and tell me what's been going on. There seems to be far more changing here than just my office. What's initiated all this?"

Melissa sat down on the chair in front of David's desk. She put down the small notepad and pen she'd been carrying and placed her hands in her lap.

"Well, it all began when I went for a walk in the park when you'd been taken into hospital. Lucy called me to say you wouldn't be coming in and that you'd had a heart attack. I told the team and we decided to shut the depot for the day. Everyone was concerned, David, and they didn't feel they could work. Poor old Eric was beside himself with worry, so I sent everyone home, put some signs on the doors explaining that this was due to an unexpected illness and that we were shut for the day. We didn't know if you were even going to pull through."

"Blimey," said David. "I didn't think you all cared so much!"

"Of course we do David. Anyway, I decided to go for a walk through the park to clear my head. While I was passing the cemetery, I noticed a tall man standing next to a gravestone in the area dedicated to cremations. I didn't think anything of it, but the man called out to me and asked me how you were. I thought it was a strange question, but realising he must know you, I thought I should let him know you weren't well. He said his name was Samuel and that you'd met him and helped him a little while ago. He wanted you to know he was going back to church and had found his faith once again. He said he'd come to the depot a few times to tell you but decided not to disturb you as you always seemed to have someone with you. He recognised me as he'd seen me through the windows and he'd also chatted with Eric."

David knew Melissa was talking about Samuel Hutchinson and he felt happy to know Samuel had found his faith once more.

"Did Samuel say anything else Mel?"

Melissa cocked her head to one side. "Well, yes. And that's the strange part. He looked at me and said life was like the big chessboard in the park. You know, the one with the huge pieces that you need two people to move. Anyway, I said goodbye to Samuel and continued my walk and when I got to the big chessboard, there were two people who appeared to be playing the game. One was clearly a vagrant with a walking stick and the other was a smart old man in a pinstripe suit. It was completely bizarre. As I walked past them, the old man was telling the vagrant lady, who he called Mary, that it might be David's move. Because your name was mentioned, my ears pricked up."

David was intrigued. "What else did the old man say?"

"He told the lady that the game of chess was like life and that David has his pieces and the other pieces were the Governor's. I have no idea who the Governor is, but he said that you would play your pieces and the Governor would play his. He said that each time you move a piece in your life, the Governor responds with a move and each time the Governor moves a piece, you must respond, and that's how the game of life moves on. I stopped walking and starting to watch them from a little distance away and I'm certain he knew I was there, as he kept looking over at me. He then said that sometimes you can feel like you're losing your game of life and you can get stuck. He went across to the chess-board and moved his queen across in front of Mary's king and shouted out 'check'. He then said this was all part of the Governor's game to force you to move. And when you do, the game continues."

David was enthralled by the metaphor of the game of chess and understood completely what Mel was telling him.

"As I walked away from the game, he raised his voice even more as if I was meant to hear him. He said that when we're in check, there is always somewhere to go and a move we can make. It might not always be the one we'd chose, but there must be a way out, as it's the rules of the game we're playing. He said the only time the game ends is when it's checkmate and this means the game's over and we go and see the Governor."

"Crikey, that's quite a message. Do you think he was talking about me Mel?"

"I don't think so David, I'm sure it was just a coincidence. But I did think about you, your heart attack and whether your life needed to change by taking some action in a specific direction. I started thinking about my own life too and perhaps whether I needed to take some action to help you.

As I walked away from the two strange chess players, the old man lifted his hat to acknowledge me. It was a bit spooky to be honest to watch the dirty old lady and the smart old man, but I felt this eerie sense of complete calmness. It was as if time stood still while I was watching them. Anyway, as I headed back to my bus stop, I realised I could spend my time worrying about you, the business, my job and what it all means, or I could just get on and do something different. So, I did."

Melissa smiled at David, almost embarrassed as if hiding a secret.

"Gosh Mel, what did you do?"

"Well, I decided the first step was to help you to get organised. It's what I'm good at and I love it too. It's something that's always been important to me and to be honest David, I think it's my calling in life!"

David laughed. "What? You think your calling in life is to be organised?"

"Not quite David," said Mel, "but I do think for me to be truly me, I must build my life more around the things which are important to me. I've thought about these things and I've realised I enjoy helping people. I like to feel useful, and tidiness and being organised are also key values of mine. I recognised this could perhaps help you to be less stressed and more in control. So, I came in a little early the last couple of mornings and tackled your office. I'd have preferred to get your permission, but I also know if I'd asked you, you probably wouldn't have let me do it. So, you being in hospital for a few days gave me the opportunity to do what I do best and this is the result." Mel waved her hands around the office to show David what she had been doing.

"It's amazing Mel and I'm truly grateful. I would never have had the drive or enthusiasm to get on top of all this, and I hate filing as you know!"

David and Melissa laughed together and whilst they'd worked together for a long time, laughter was a rare occurrence and for them both, it felt good. They chatted about where Melissa had put important files and she walked around the office highlighting what she'd done. David was amazed at just how much she had done in such a short space of time.

"But when you do what you love, your work loves you back," said Melissa.

"Ha! Who told you that Mel?"

"No-one David, I just realised while I was tidying up, loving what I was doing, the results were there for themselves. When I was doing work I loved, the work got easier and the results were better. Plus, there's something else I need to tell you David."

"Go on then," said David, wondering what was coming next.

"Well, I hope this is OK," said Melissa sheepishly, "but I was looking through some of your clients in your prospect folder and I noticed some correspondence from you to Richard Bailey at K. Bailey and Sons. You said in your last letter to him that you would follow up but there was no further correspondence since."

"Yeah, I'd meant to call him," said David, "but as he'd already knocked me back once, I decided there was no point in hassling him. I think we are too small for them to consider us as a supplier for their major projects."

"That's where you're wrong David. I called him and explained to his secretary you'd been taken into hospital and I was following up on your behalf. She put me straight through."

"Crikey Mel, what did you say as I often struggle to get past his secretary, whatever her name is."

Melissa scowled at him. "Maybe that's why you never got past her if you don't even know her name. She said her name was Maria and she'd only just started working for Richard, but she was lovely, and we chatted about you. She seemed to know who you were, which was rather odd, but she put me through to Richard and I told him who I was and why I was calling."

Mell shuffled in her chair as if uncomfortable about what she was about to say next. "And then I just asked him," she said.

"Asked him what?"

"Why they hadn't awarded us a contract."

David spun around in his chair, laughing. Richard Bailey was one of the most difficult, direct and blunt people he'd met in business. Many said he was ruthless and not like his father Keith Bailey, who had been very popular with his clients and customers. Richard was a different animal and didn't take kindly to being challenged or his decisions questioned and yet Melissa, who'd never had a day's sales training in her life, had asked Richard a very direct question.

"How did he respond Mel? I'm amazed you were so direct with him."

"Interesting David, as I remembered you'd told me he was very direct, so I thought he'd respect me more if I was equally direct, but respectful. He just laughed and told me he loved my direct approach."

"What happened then? This sounds fascinating!"

"Well, he explained he thought we couldn't cope with the volume of parts we'd need to supply. But then he went on to say it was a pure coincidence I'd called as he'd just got off the phone from his preferred supplier, who'd let him down on several occasions. He called it something like 'synchronicity' which didn't mean much to me, but he seemed very interested in the timing of my call."

"Wow Mel, this is amazing!" David could feel his pulse increasing and his heart was starting to race. But this time it didn't feel scary – it felt exciting.

"We chatted about terms, pricing and supply and then we agreed we would be trialled as a new supplier for 3 months. If we could cope with their volumes and delivered a good service, we could become their preferred supplier within 6 months."

"I'm amazed Mel. What could the business be worth to us?"

"About a million pounds a year."

"What?" exclaimed David, pushing himself away from his desk.

Mel remained calm in the face of David's excitement.

"Yes, up to one million pounds a year."

David looked at Mel and smiled. "And you did all that in one phone call? How did you do it Mel?"

"Just by being me David. I didn't think about trying to be clever or salesy, I just spoke to him in a way I thought he'd respect and that drew on my strengths. You've always said I could be a bit direct at times but perhaps on this occasion, me being me worked! Perhaps because I was just being authentic, I was relaxed and comfortable chatting to him. Another example of if you love your work, your work loves you back I guess."

"I'm staggered Mel and of course, incredibly grateful. Maybe I should put you in charge of the business more often!"

"Well.... funny you should say that, as I've been thinking," said Mel.

"Oh right, so there's even more to tell then Mel?"

There was a knock at the door. It was Billy.

"Sorry to interrupt you both but John Benjamin from Smithwood Piping is here to see Melissa."

"Thanks Billy," said Mel. "Tell him I'll be with him in a couple of minutes."

"OK. Will do," said Billy and he closed the door.

"Can we speak later about the other stuff David as I really need to speak to John. I've got some good news for him too."

"What's the good news Mel?"

"Well, John supported us when he came in a few days ago with the extra credit didn't he? I've checked out Smithwood and they are a secure and robust company with good values. I'm going to ask him to supply the fittings for the Bailey's contract. Could be a nice reward for their support for us. Do you agree?"

David did agree. He was also deeply moved by how much Melissa had stepped up during the short time he'd been away. He was also amazed how a new contract which could save the business had come about. He was warmed by the feeling that young John Benjamin would quickly get a reward for his willingness to help them.

Melissa left David and walked over to meet John. David noticed the warmth of their greeting, which was at odds with the last time John had been to see him. Melissa had been positively frosty towards him and yet here they were, greeting each other like old friends.

David sat at his desk wondering what had changed to make things turn around so quickly.

Then inside his head he heard the voice again.

"Everything's changed," was all it said.

13.

David spent the morning going through his emails and understanding the new filing system Melissa had put in place for him. She had clearly spent more time than her usual hours at work, as she had completely revamped almost every part of his office. Even a couple of pictures had been replaced and on the wall opposite his desk a picture of a lion roaring had been placed, with words across the bottom of the picture saying, *'Rise up and be the best you can be because your world is waiting for you'.*

There was something deeply reassuring about those words, confirming much of what the previous few days had taught him. He also noticed the words 'be the best' within the sentence too, which prompted him to spend some time browsing the website of the 'Be the Best' conference. Despite initially grimacing at some of the imagery of fists punching the air and men and women seeming to be hysterical in the audience, David found himself drawn deeper into the website. He read some of the personal stories of the speakers who were on each day of the conference, and just as Lucy had suggested, some of them had endured experiences like his own. Some had stories of difficult childhoods; some had faced business and personal failures; and some had come through challenging endurance tests. But each of them appeared ready to share their stories to help others. While he didn't recognise any of the names of the speakers, he did recognise some of the experiences they each described as the basis of their talks.

David's concentration was broken by another knock at his office door. It was John Benjamin, who poked his head around the door and smiled at David.

"Hi David, have you got a moment?"

"Yes John, please do come in."

John came into the office, trusted pilot case in hand and dressed as smartly as ever. After a strong handshake, he sat down in the chair in front of David's desk.

"Gosh David, it sounds like you had a close call. How are you feeling?"

"I'm good thanks John, and glad to be back at work. It seems Melissa has been busy whilst I've been away!"

"Yes David, she's been incredible. She called me a couple of days ago to tell me you were in hospital and we chatted about the new credit terms I'd set up for you. Then today, she's just invited me to tender our fittings for the new contract she thinks you're going to get from Bailey's. It's incredible David and just shows how quickly things can turn around eh?"

"Sure John, I was amazed and to be honest it hasn't quite sunk in yet. I went into hospital with a business struggling to pay its bills and have come out with a business expanding in a direction I never thought possible."

"When you allow people to do what they do best, give them the trust to make good decisions and step back, amazing things can happen David."

David's 'stepping back' hadn't been a conscious decision but had been forced upon him by the heart attack, but he was certainly happy it had happened. He gulped as a wave of emotion swept over him. He thought about Peter and how he'd have been just a bit younger than John Benjamin sat in front of him now. John reminded him of Peter, and he would've been proud if Peter had helped someone, just like John had helped him. John broke the moment of silence.

"I wanted to tell you I met Michael again too. Can I tell you about it?"

David leant forward in his chair and put his arms on his desk. "Yes, please do."

"Well, it was a few hours after I'd had the call from Melissa about you. I was at the same careers event I'd attended before when I'd met him but this time, I was manning our stand. We wanted to tell the young people about the career opportunities in our business and I was really looking forward to it. As soon as I walked into the room, I saw him. He was in deep conversation with a young chap who was nodding away and as I walked towards him to say hello, he turned around and looked straight at me. It was quite spooky. I knew he was giving the young chap the same advice he'd given me because his last words to him were 'and remember it all starts with love'. You and I both know that phrase don't we David?"

"Yes, John, we do. Go on."

"Well, it got really odd. Without any introductions at all, he told me not to worry about you, that everything had been sorted and you'd be out of hospital within a day. I hadn't even mentioned your name, but he knew you were in hospital. I asked him if he knew Melissa or if anyone had called him and he just said that Mary had been to see you and I didn't need to worry. And then he said the strangest thing. He said some good news was on the way which would change everything. He then touched my shoulder and moved away. I barely had a moment to ask him anything and as I looked around, I couldn't see him anywhere in the room. He must've left immediately, so I went across to the young chap he'd been speaking to, a smashing lad called Kevin Charfield, and we chatted for ages. Michael had told him exactly what he'd told me, including the importance of finding your purpose. And do you know what David? Kevin starts work with us next week. I talked about him to Chris, our sales director, and we agreed to get him in for interview. We did so the following day and now just three days later, it's all sorted. It's as if some weird synchronicity has stepped in."

David was pleased and reassured in equal measure. He was delighted John had found a recruit who would no doubt become a protégé of his. But he was also reassured that Michael had known about his heart attack. He still didn't fully understand who Michael was but his presence in his life felt comforting.

"Well John, I'm truly delighted for you. It seems that me being ill has had a positive impact all round!"

"Maybe this is how the world works David. Perhaps there's some cosmic order balancing our lives in some way."

"Blimey! Cosmic order? That's a bit heavy John, but maybe there's a grain of truth in there somewhere. Whatever's been going on, it all seems to be for the good, so I'm happy with accepting there's something out there to help us!"

"I'd better be getting along now David. I just wanted to pop in and see how you were after your scare. I'm delighted to see you looking forwards now too. I'll come in and see you once we've got these new contracts sorted. And I'm grateful for this fantastic additional business David. Thank you."

David stood up to shake John's hand. "It's Mel you need to thank John, she's the one who pulled it all together. But you reached out a hand of support to me first, so maybe what goes around comes around?"

John shook David's hand vigorously. "Indeed David, maybe that's how all this stuff works. See you soon anyway."

John left the office and David watched him walk across the depot floor, waving and high-fiving people as he left. He was an inspirational young man and David wondered whether he'd attended any of the conferences or read any of the books Lucy had become hooked upon.

David went back to his computer and the website for the 'Be the Best' conference. He started to read more about the event and what he and Lucy could expect. He realised maybe he was getting hooked on the idea of being the best.

The day had flown by and the trade counter was busy. Several people enquired about David, particularly his loyal and long-standing customers, so David found himself constantly interrupted. By the time it came to leave, he'd hardly touched some of the tasks Melissa had left for him. But David felt he was running a different business. His eyes had been opened to new possibilities and opportunities and it felt good.

The journey home felt different too. Before his heart attack, David's body had been full of stress and worry. He had constant backache and despite his regular walks through Highgate Park, he'd struggled to free himself from the negative thoughts filling his mind daily.

The light was fading, and the clouds looked full of snow, creating an eerie glow that suggested it was going to be a cold and possibly snowy evening. As he pulled into his estate he thought about Peter. He decided to park the car at home and head over to the cemetery to visit Peter's stone. He wanted to talk to his son about what had been happening, including the good news he'd received.

By the time he reached the gates into Highgate Park and began the walk towards the cemetery, the light was fading even more, making the park a quiet but desolate place. Shadows formed around bushes and trees and David considered heading home and postponing his visit until the following day when the light would be more reassuring. But he found his feet stepping forwards in a mind of their own and soon, he stood at the entrance to the cemetery. In the far corner, near to where Peter's stone was laid, he could see a glow from what appeared to be a head torch. It was moving around and David was worried someone was interfering with his son's plot. His pace quickened as he walked towards the glow and the person who appeared to be kneeling beneath it. As he got closer, he could see it was a man in a long coat, on his knees, placing flowers on the gravestone next to Peter's. It was Samuel.

"Hey Samuel, how are you?" said David, relieved the strange night-time visitor was nothing more sinister. Samuel stood up and greeted David warmly.

"Hello David, how lovely to see you. Let me turn off this head torch, it must be blinding you."

"Why are you here in the dark?" asked David.

"I could ask you the same question David."

"Ha, I guess so Samuel but why are you here?"

"I wanted to come and tell Lucia I've rediscovered my faith and it was all because of you."

"Gosh, that's great to hear Samuel but I'm not sure I did much really."

"Oh yes you did, and you also came to me in a dream the night after you had your heart attack. When we met in the church, I was about as far away as I could be from God, but you seemed to spark something in me to start praying again. Then I had this vivid dream where you were drinking tea in a hospital bed and chatting to a tea lady called Mary. In the dream, Mary turned to me and offered me a drink too. She said it contained the cup of life and I simply needed to start drinking from it once more. She also said it was my move on my chessboard of life. I had to decide whether to drink from the cup again. She also said you'd be fine. Then I woke up. The following day, I saw your assistant Mel as she walked through the cemetery and she told me about your heart attack. I told her what Mary had told me in the dream and that she had to make her move. I hope she has."

"Gosh Samuel, she certainly has made a move, she's been transforming my business whilst I've been in hospital. She said it couldn't have happened if I hadn't been taken ill. And your dream, the bit with Mary offering you a cup of tea? I'm curious, what did it mean to you?"

Samuel reached out his hand and placed it on David's arm. "That was the simple bit David. I needed to drink again from the cup, so I started praying again. And Jesus spoke to me in a way I'd not heard for a long time. He welcomed me home David and told me he'd always been there. He said it was my move and I was the one who needed to choose to follow him once more."

"I'm pleased for you Samuel, I really am. Have you told Lucia all about it?"

"I have and it's made me feel closer to her somehow. When I lost my faith there was nothing to believe in; nothing would reassure me she was still alive. Then I remembered Jesus was alive and that if I could talk to him, I could talk to her too. I've contacted the bishop and asked to be re-considered for work. It's like my life is starting all over again David."

The two men chatted more about what had been happening to them both. David didn't mention Mary's visit to him in hospital. The hospital staff had insisted no-one had visited him, so David wondered if they'd both dreamed the same dream.

The light continued to fade and the temperature dropped. Soon clouds of vapour were being created through their constant talking. David realised he hadn't been talking to Peter but figured he could hear what he'd been telling Samuel.

Their talk was broken by a deep voice bellowing from the darkness some distance away.

"What are you doing by there?" It was an accent David recognised and through the darkness, he could see a torch being waved at them and the familiar Welsh accent of George the gardener who David had met before. "Now then, you shouldn't be by here this time of night, haven't you got homes to go to David and Samuel?"

Samuel stepped back. "How do you know our names and who are you?"

"The name's George Jones, park gardener and I'm in charge of this here garden."

"But this is a cemetery. The gardens are over there," said Samuel, pointing over towards the park.

"Ah yes, but it's all part of my garden boyo and even at this time of night, there's still weeds to be pulling out isn't there?"

David reached out his hand.

"Hello George, nice to see you again."

"You too boyo. At this time of night when the light is low and there's less traffic about, sound travels along the ground. I could hear your voices, so I came over to see what was occurring. And I need to let you both know something too. When you've cleared away the weeds and planted new seeds, you need to nurture them. They're fragile see. Easy to be knocked over or suffocated by them darned weeds that always seem to be growing somewhere. Watch out for them. The weeds will often grow fastest just after you've planted new seeds in your fertile soil. That's all I'm saying to you two. Now get yourselves off home before you freeze to death out here."

George turned and walked away, lifting his cap and he soon disappeared behind a bush, although it seemed to David that George walked straight into a shadow.

Samuel was staring after George too and for a moment there was a silence between them.

"What was all that about?" said Samuel, flicking on his head torch once more and shining it in the direction where George had been walking. "And who on earth was he?"

"That's George, the park gardener, I've met him before Samuel. He's the one who guided me to the church I told you about."

"But there aren't any park gardeners," said Samuel. "The park is maintained by a local council contractor. There haven't been park gardeners for the last five years and certainly none who would be out weeding at nearly 7 o'clock in the evening! So, who on earth was he? And where did he go? It was if he walked into a shadow and disappeared."

"Do you believe that God sends people to help us Samuel?"

"That's quite a question David. But I know that God is within all of us so that sometimes in our lives we find ourselves offering help to others and at other times, we're the ones who receive the help. And as God orchestrates everything, I guess you could say that He does send us people to help us."

"I know it seems crazy Samuel, but the last few weeks have been strange for me. I keep meeting people who seem to want to help and give me important messages. Even in hospital, I met people with important things to say, as if they are 'orchestrated' in some way, leading me somewhere, but I'm not exactly sure where now. Do you think guardian angels exist Samuel?"

"Maybe we're all angels in God's kingdom, David, but sometimes we fail to see it. I believe God does send people to give us important messages at certain times in our lives, and maybe it doesn't matter whether you believe in guardian angels or not. What's more important is that we take on board the messages we receive, wherever they've come from."

"Yes, perhaps you're right Samuel. What do you think George was trying to tell us?"

"That's interesting David. It felt like a warning to me. Perhaps when things appear to be looking up, we're more vulnerable to some of the negative forces. I know the Bible warns of this is in the parable of the sower. Maybe it's easy to doubt that things can get better when they've been difficult for so long. I know I've learned to cope with the empty space Lucia left behind, and I've got used to the feeling. Feeling happy isn't something I'm used to but since I've reconnected to my faith, it's certainly felt like happiness, even though I've doubted at times whether it will last. Perhaps these doubts are the weeds George was warning us about?"

"You could be right Samuel. Let's be on our guard and keep believing happiness can be permanent rather than temporary."

"Yes David, happiness may come and go, but joy can be permanent when we're certain everything happens to us is for our greater good, even when it doesn't seem so at the time."

David remembered what John had said in his office.

"Well, there's certainly some greater good to come out of my heart attack, Samuel, so maybe there is some master plan to all this. Anyway, I can feel the chill creeping into my bones so perhaps it's time to leave this place and head home to the warm!"

The men hugged each other, said their goodbyes and headed in different directions out of the cemetery. David was aware of the shapes and shadows lurking in the dark but kept his eyes firmly fixed on the lamps lighting up the park just beyond the cemetery. He walked briskly to keep warm and was relieved to see the glow from the lights behind the curtains. His home looked even more inviting and cosy than he previously remembered, and he looked forward to telling Lucy the great news about the business.

14.

David walked up the drive to the house, letting himself in.

"Hi, I'm home," he called out to anyone who might hear him.

"Hi honey," called Lucy from the kitchen. David walked down the hall and rushed up to Lucy and, picking her up, kissed her fully on the lips.

"Gosh, what's got into you?" asked Lucy. "Put me down before you give yourself another heart attack! How was your day then? Has the business survived whilst you've been away?" Lucy turned back to the pan on the cooker from where an amazing smell of chilli con carne was drifting across the kitchen.

"It was only a week or so Lucy, but I can't believe what's happened. How about this? While I was in hospital Mel secured a million-pound contract with Bailey's!"

"What?" said Lucy, spinning around to face David. "What do you mean?"

"Well, it's simple really. Mel started to go through the outstanding correspondence on my desk and came across a letter from Bailey's saying we hadn't been successful in our bid. It was one of the final blows that made me feel we weren't going to make it Lucy. But Mel simply rang up and spoke directly to Richard Bailey. I'd been trying to reach him for weeks, but Mel got put straight through. It appears their current supplier has let them down so he gave us a chance to prove we can supply the fittings. It's worth about a million pounds a year Lucy and secures the future of the business. I can't believe it!"

"Maybe you should be ill more often if this is going to be the result!" said Lucy. "Good on Mel. I always said to you she was capable of more than just the admin."

"The funny thing Lucy is she found one of your motivational CDs in my drawer and she listened to it out of curiosity. It was Robin Anton too, who's speaking at the conference. She said it encouraged her to be her best. She also met Samuel Hutchinson as she walked through Highgate Park and he told her to make a move for her career too. It's all very spooky and weird Lucy. I just popped over the see Peter and to tell him all about what has been going on, and Samuel was putting some flowers on Lucia's stone. We chatted about what had been happening and he told me he'd rediscovered his faith. There's a lot of positive things happening Lucy. I definitely think we've turned a corner!"

Lucy placed her hands on her hips and took an envelope out of the pocket of her apron. "I think you'd better sit down." David sat down on one of the kitchen chairs. "I'm sorry to burst your bubble honey but this came for you today. I opened it as I didn't want you to worry. I want you to get better and not have any stress but I'm sorry, you need to know about this straightaway. There's no easy way to say this, but the bank wants to repossess the house. It seems we've not been keeping up with the mortgage payments. Why didn't you tell me?"

The atmosphere in the room had changed in an instant from one of euphoria to one of doom and gloom. David felt a weight on his shoulders again and his chest tightened. He looked at the letter which was from the bank holding the mortgage on the house. It simply stated it was commencing legal proceedings to repossess their property.

"I'm so sorry Lucy. I thought I'd be able to turn things around before it got too heavy. But I think I was just burying my head in the sand. I'll call them tomorrow and see if I can buy us more time. Now we have this new contract, I may be able to draw a salary again from the business and maybe we can start paying back some of the arrears."

"Hi Dad," said Annabel, bouncing into the kitchen in her usual manner. "Have you been taking it easy then like the doctors said? What's the matter Dad? Do you feel unwell again?" Annabel placed her hand on David's shoulder. "Mum, Dad looks really pale again. Should we call a doctor?"

"I'm fine Annabel," said David. "Just dealing with some financial stuff, that's all."

"But I could hear you telling Mum about the new contract. That's good news isn't it?"

"Yes, it is Annabel, but the bank is getting a bit jumpy, as I haven't paid the mortgage properly for a little while."

"They'll be fine. Just call them up and be smiley and friendly and they're bound to want to help."

"It's not that simple Annabel," said Lucy, not appreciating her usual brand of optimism.

"Hey Dad, you OK?" said Georgia, entering the kitchen and shuffling around the table to sit down. "What's up? You look like death. Sorry Dad – you know what I mean."

"Dad's not been paying enough of the mortgage," said Annabel. "And now the bank has overreacted and is putting Dad under pressure. He doesn't need this Mum. Is there anything we can do to help?"

"Just tell them to bugger off," mumbled Georgia. "Banks are run by computers, so just tell them you'll pay when you're good and ready. Bloody hate banks."

"Sit down girls, this is serious," said Lucy.

Annabel sat down next to Georgia, and Lucy slipped onto a chair next to David.

"Dad's not been able to draw a wage from the business for a while, so he hasn't been paying enough of the mortgage. I didn't know, as he kept it a secret from me but I'm not going to make a big thing out of that now. We need to look forwards and not backwards. We must face up to the fact that we might need to sell the house to pay off the arrears and move into something smaller."

"Doesn't bother me," said Georgia.

"If it will help ease the pressure on Dad, then I'm fine Mum," said Annabel.

David was silent and he could feel the weeds growing in his mind. He'd failed his family. Despite the good news today, the past was catching up with him and he couldn't outrun it anymore. He had to face the consequences of his inability to manage his family business through the recession. He'd buried his head in the sand and now his family were going to suffer the consequences.

"I'm sorry, I've let you all down," said David. "I've failed in the most basic role a father can have, namely, to provide safety and shelter for his family."

"Don't be an arse, Dad," said Georgia. "Being a dad is a lot more than the size of house we live in. I couldn't give a toss where we live as long as you're OK. We nearly lost you, so stop worrying about the house. I've never liked it much anyway."

Georgia's bluntness was somehow refreshing for David and he smiled at her. "Thanks love, I appreciate that."

"Don't worry Dad, you'll be able to sort something out," said Annabel.

"There was some good news today too girls," said Lucy. "The business won a big new contract thanks to Melissa

Smith." Lucy returned to the chilli and the pot of rice bubbling on the stove.

"Yes, while I was off, she telephoned a big customer. A potential customer really, and she asked them why we hadn't been awarded a contract. After some discussion, they have agreed to trial us as a supplier. It could be worth a million pounds a year."

"Wow Dad, that's amazing!" said Annabel. "Surely that will satisfy the banks won't it?"

"Banks are bastards Annabel – they won't care," said Georgia.

"Language Georgia, please," said Lucy.

"Well it's true Mum. Sarah Lewis was a friend of mine at school and I remember her dad had a similar problem and even though his circumstances changed, they went through with repossessing their house. They ended up in a much smaller rented house. So no, I'm sorry Mum, but banks are bastards – period."

"Listen girls," said David, "I've had a good day today and I'm not going to let this letter from the bank spoil it. I want to enjoy this chilli as I didn't get the chance to finish the previous spicy meal your mum cooked. I ended up in hospital, so let's just eat together and celebrate I'm even here to receive this letter."

"Blimey, makes a change David," said Lucy. "And I totally agree. You must've had a good day today. Let's enjoy the chilli."

David remembered what George has said to him and Samuel. "Someone said something to me today about being careful when things are going well. He said negative thoughts can easily creep in, so I'm not going to let this letter spoil my day." David looked around at his family.

"Thanks George," he thought to himself.

15.

David slept restlessly. Dreams of weeds strangling him and his house falling down were all figments of an imagination stimulated by the previous day's events. When he awoke, it was dark outside and chilly in the bedroom. Lucy was still asleep, and the alarm clock showed 5.11am. After shuffling around in bed for about 10 minutes, he decided to get up and go for a walk to clear his head and get ready for the day. He wondered if he'd meet the mysterious path-sweeper again.

He picked up his jogging trousers and trainers from the bedroom floor where he'd last left them and tiptoed down the landing and down the stairs. He pulled on his trousers and sat on the bottom stair to put on his trainers. He remembered when he'd sat in the same spot on the anniversary of Peter's birthday, when all the chance meetings with strangers had begun. Since then, he'd managed to squeeze in a heart attack and a visit to hospital too.

He grabbed his coat and headed for the door, which he opened and pulled too gently. As he turned to walk away from the house, he felt the biting cold. It was still dark, with little sign of the sunrise or the coming of spring, and his breath generated vapours of steam as he started to walk.

As he arrived at the park, he heard the familiar sound of the robin tweeting somewhere nearby. As he pushed open the gate, the friendly robin swooped down and landed on the top of the gate, right in front of David's eyes. The little bird stuck out its red chest and tweeted away at David as if it was asking where he'd been. The robin cocked its head from side to side and then leapt from the gate, heading off in an unknown direction.

There was a hint of fog in the air, drifting over and around the trees. As David walked and the ever-present London traffic pierced the silence, he began to think about what to do about the house and whether he should sell up or see if he could come to an arrangement with the bank.

He quickened his pace to get some warmth into his body and more blood pumping around his heart. As he rounded a bend, he noticed a familiar figure sitting on the bench ahead of him in the early morning gloom and walked up to him.

"Hello Michael," said David, thrusting his hand towards Michael who immediately stood up and warmly shook his hand.

"Good to see you too David. How've you been?"

David sat down on the bench next to Michael and told him what had happened since he'd first met him, who listened intently without interrupting.

"You can see it's been a bumpy but fascinating ride since we met."

Michael was rubbing his chin, contemplating what to say next. In the silence, the breathing and accompanying vapour trails were all anyone passing would have noticed.

"I think you've received some excellent guidance David and it seems you've really taken stock of your life and what's important to you. Now comes the tricky part."

David's heart sank, just like it did the first time he'd met Michael. But this time, David didn't know why. He felt a sense of foreboding, as if Michael was about to burst the bubble in which he'd been operating these last few weeks.

"Do you believe everything happens for your greater good David?"

"I'm not sure what you mean. I can see that some good has come out of the difficulties of the past week or so but that's just coincidence isn't it?"

"I thought so," said Michael, gazing into the distance. "Your belief system isn't strong enough yet David. You still think you can fix everything yourself, don't you?"

"No, I don't Michael. I know I needed help and I've accepted some, just like you told me to. But I do think that my path ahead is for me to step into. You told Mel that I had to move a piece on my chessboard and I'm ready to do this now Michael."

"I'm glad that you took her advice David and yes, of course, your new path is set now. But sometimes it's hard to know if you're at the end of something or the beginning of the next move. Be ready for the unexpected David."

Michael got up from the bench and started to walk away. "Good day to you David and may God go with you." He lifted his hat from his head, just as he had before and continued to walk into the distance.

David remained on the bench, taking on board what Michael had said. He wondered how he could be ready for things that are unexpected? It was a puzzling paradox. He wondered if he should just let go of the house and allow the bank to take it from them. Or perhaps he should ring up an estate agent and put it up for sale. At least he'd get to keep the equity. It was all confusing and draining, and he could feel his energy fading.

The light was beginning to emerge in the east side of the park and David got up and headed back towards the edge of the park and his home. Other people, mainly with dogs, were beginning to enter the park and David realised it was the dog walking hour where many residents walked their dogs before breakfast. As he reached the edge of the park and his gate, the robin was back once more. But this time it was silent, just watching David as he left the park.

He walked back up the road through his estate to his house and as he approached the front drive he stopped. He could feel the weeds of negativity in his mind growing once more as he looked at the house he and Lucy had worked hard to afford for the family; the sacrifices they made as they'd saved up for the deposit and the money they'd spent since on keeping the decoration in good order; the landscaped garden and welcoming family home. He considered the impact of losing it all and the dark shadows within his mind started to grow, seeping into every pore of his body, pulling him downwards and backwards into the spiral of despair he'd felt just a few weeks ago.

"Hey Dad! What are you doing?" It was Annabel who'd opened her bedroom window and was clearly wondering what her dad was doing staring at the house. "Are you coming in for some breakfast? It's freezing out there!"

"Just coming love." He walked up the drive and through the front door which Annabel had dashed downstairs to open for him.

"How was your walk?" asked Lucy, walking down the stairs as David removed his trainers in the hall.

"It was fine thanks. Just trying to clear my head a little for the day ahead."

David headed for the kitchen, hoping Lucy wouldn't ask him anything else about his walk as he really didn't want to mention Michael and what he'd said. He just wanted some breakfast and to be left alone with his thoughts.

"I've been thinking David," said Lucy, as she followed him into the kitchen. "Maybe we should cancel our tickets to the 'Be the Best' conference. If we need to pay the mortgage, I'm not sure we can be spending money on feel-good events."

"You might be right Lucy. It does seem a little extravagant, particularly with the hotel costs too. I'll ring up today and cancel the hotel and I'll see if I can get a refund on the tickets."

Lucy sat down opposite David at the kitchen table. "Are you OK love? You seem a bit down this morning?"

"I'm fine. Just got a fair bit on my mind with the new contract at work." David hoped his response would put Lucy off the scent. He wasn't feeling fine at all. The darkness of depression was pushing inwards and beginning to envelop him. It was like cold fingers running all over his body and he recognised the feelings only too well. Maybe it would've been better if his heart attack had been more serious.

"Well, make sure you focus on the new contract today and maybe let me deal with the bank. You've got enough on your plate, so give me the details and I'll call them, OK?"

"No, it's my mess Lucy and I need to sort it. I'll call them today."

"If you're sure."

"I am."

But David wasn't sure at all. He wasn't sure about anything. Losing the house they'd worked hard for was always a possibility, but he'd hoped he'd be able to turn the business around before it became an inevitability. But time had run out. The irony of the new contract arriving just too late was painful to consider.

David finished his cereal and Lucy busied herself making lunch for the girls and watching breakfast television. The banality of the news items and features on the TV frustrated him, as if they didn't reflect the seriousness of his own situation. The latest love triangle involving some celebrity just didn't seem to matter and he could feel anger rising in his chest. Or was it the chest pain he'd felt before? He took a deep breath, rose from the table, placed his breakfast bowl in the dishwasher, kissed Lucy on the cheek and headed for the door.

"Have a good day! Love you!" Lucy called whilst still transfixed by the latest celebrity gossip on the TV.

"Will do. Love you too."

David grabbed his coat and headed for the door towards a future that was as uncertain in his mind as ever.

By the time he arrived at the depot, the short drive had begun to clear his head a little and the gloom he'd felt earlier had started to lift. Eric was in the yard, ready and willing as always to greet him with a smile and this morning with a salute.

"Morning guvnor. How's you keeping this fine morning?"

"Great, thanks Eric, how are you today?"

"Could be betta me old china. Had some news this mornin' I'd like to share with you."

"Sure, go ahead. What's up."

"Well it's me nephew you see. He's asked me to help him out a few days a week at his car valeting business and you know I love to clean the motors, so I said I would. Is that going to be alright guvnor? You don't really need me here as much nowadays and although I ain't earning a fortune, you probably could do with me off the wage bill and that. He'd like me to start next week. Would that be alright guvnor?"

David felt a strange mix of sadness and relief. Sad because Eric was part of the furniture and the only remaining link to his Dad who'd started the business, but also relieved as he wouldn't need to make him redundant in the future.

"Of course, Eric. We'll all be really sad to see you go, but I'm delighted for you and your nephew."

"Well it will be a sad day when I walk out those gates for the last time. I remember meeting your dad for the first time, when he told me if I worked hard, I'd have a job for life, and he weren't wrong, was he? But all good things must come to an end, don't they? As my old dad used to say to me, endings are just the beginnings of something new."

"Maybe so Eric. I'll sort out your final wage packet with Mel and we'll have a bit of a get-together on Friday to say cheerio and good luck, shall we?"

"Nah. I don't want fuss guvnor. Just happy to slip away quietly and take my memories with me. No need to make a song and dance about it."

David shook Eric's hand and headed into the depot where some of the staff were arriving and setting up stock. The trade counter already had a few customers waiting and Billy was busy serving them. As David walked towards his office, Billy acknowledged him with a brief wave but got back to serving the customers immediately. Billy was the future of the business whilst Eric was a nod to the past. It made David think about endings and beginnings again and how they were often linked.

David sat down at his desk just as Melissa knocked on the office door. "Can I have a quick word David?"

"Of course, do come in Melissa, and how are you this morning?"

"I'm fine thanks," she said, keen to get down to business. "I've been doing some cashflow forecasts based on the income from the new contract and it's really positive David. If we get paid on time, and I've put some pretty tough terms into the contract, then I believe this can genuinely turn the business around. You won't need to make anyone redundant either. In fact, we're going to need more staff to cope with the extra work involved, so I've factored in two more warehouse staff and a new admin person to help me. I hope that's OK David?"

David was still thinking about endings and beginnings and hadn't fully taken in what Melissa had said. He was wondering if selling the house might be a beginning rather than an ending.

"David? Is that OK?"

"Erm, yes Mel, thanks for doing the numbers, I'll look through them shortly once I've had my first coffee. Need to get the brain cells warmed up!"

"OK then. Can you look through the cashflow forecast and my assumptions when you've woken up a little please?" Melissa placed some papers onto David's desk, clearly slightly miffed he hadn't been more enthusiastic.

But David was preoccupied by what Eric and Billy represented. One man towards the end of his career and one at the beginning. But even Eric, who could be coming to the end of something, was also at the beginning. David could feel his mood lifting and he thought about George and how his two meetings with him had both included discussions about weeds and how they can suffocate the growth of new plants. He realised much of what he was feeling was simply created by his belief systems and how he looked at situations. Something which on one hand could look like an ending could, from another angle, look like a beginning.

David's eye caught sight of his father's picture hanging on the wall on the far side of his office. He recalled how his father would often tell him that no matter whether he saw a situation positively or negatively, he was always right, meaning that how he looked at situations would determine whether they were good or bad. And perhaps there was no such thing as good or bad, and everything was part of the 'rich tapestry of life'. David smiled at his father and was certain his father's face in the picture smiled back at him. Or maybe it was just his mind deciding to see a smile? But David knew he had to look at his own situations with his house and the new contract as neither good nor bad. For all he knew, the new contract could turn out to be a huge headache and the prospect of selling this house could give everyone a new start, particularly as they hadn't moved after Peter died, and the house did contain many memories of him.

David felt slightly lightheaded and grabbed onto the desk with both hands. Was this another heart attack? The dizziness eased and he took a few deep breaths. As his breathing settled, he noticed how some of the darkness he'd felt earlier around breakfast time had lifted and been replaced with something else. He couldn't articulate it, but he knew he felt brighter than before.

He pulled open the top drawer in his desk to search for a pen to mark Melissa's cashflow forecast. Something slid forwards and clinked against the front of the drawer. It was the medal he'd had in his pocket a while ago on the anniversary of Peter's birthday. He couldn't recall putting it into his drawer and was certain the last time he'd held it in his hand, the word on the front had been 'Love'. But this medal had the word 'Faith' on it. He picked it up and turned it over and it was the same as the other medals, with an angel on one side and a single word on the other.

As David held the angel medal in his hand he thought about his own faith and about Samuel who'd rediscovered his. David wanted to believe fate was taking a hand in his life and perhaps there was some greater intelligence having an influence. But more than this, he realised he needed faith in his own ability to resolve situations in his own life. He needed to recognise when weeds were growing in his mind and to do something about them. He understood that even if he loved his work and built his success in a way that felt authentic for him, he would still have days when doubt would creep in. Maybe he would feel less certain about things on some days and that was OK. On those days, maybe he just needed to be aware of what he was thinking and to believe in himself. After all, if he didn't believe in himself, why would anyone else?

He took the medal and placed it into his pocket. Whether it was more faith he needed or more belief, or maybe they were the same thing, he wanted to keep it close to him today. If he was going to call the bank to see what he could do about their payment arrears, he needed the faith that all would be well.

He picked up the papers Mel had prepared, and they looked good. The cashflow forecast suggested that if he could secure extended payment terms with the major suppliers, the new contract could be managed without placing a strain on cashflow. In fact, cashflow would improve, as many of the costs in the business were fixed.

David leant back in his chair and decided he would call the bank while he was feeling more positive. In his mind he imagined some weeds in his garden withering and dying and he felt even stronger.

He pulled out the letter from the bank from his briefcase and looked for the number to call. The letter was signed by Ms A Henderson, although he figured this was a fictitious person who didn't really exist in the bank. It was probably some computer-generated persona to make the contents of the letter more palatable.

David dialled the number and within three rings it was answered.

"Good morning, HSBC bank, Angela Henderson speaking, how may I help you?"

David was flabbergasted that he'd not only got straight through to someone at the bank, rather than having to choose multiple options, and even more amazed that the fictitious Ms Henderson existed.

"Good morning, Ms Anderson, my name is David Turner and I've received a letter from you about our mortgage arrears."

"That's fine Mr Turner, I just need to take you through security first OK?"

After a few questions which confirmed David's identity, Ms Henderson had satisfied her computer system and was able to discuss the mortgage.

"How can I help you today Mr Turner?"

"Well, I've received a letter notifying me you're going to commence proceedings to repossess our property due to our mortgage arrears."

"Yes, that's right; I can see you are over 6 months behind now Mr Turner, is that correct?"

"Yes, it is."

"And you've spoken to my colleagues before about a temporary arrangement for you, but this has now expired, so we were now moving to the next stage. However, we'd prefer not to pursue this course of action Mr Turner, so is there any change in your circumstances to suggest you'll be able to start paying back the arrears?"

David's mind was spinning. He hadn't considered that the bank would offer him other options or that he'd even be able to start paying back his arrears. His circumstances had changed too, with the new contract set to enable him to pay himself a salary once more. He explained this to Ms Henderson who was delighted to hear of the changing circumstances and suggested she could pause the legal proceedings for another three months and that if David recommenced paying the mortgage on a regular basis, a new arrangement could be put in place to deal with the arrears.

The phone call ended with an agreement to speak again in three months' time but for now, the legal proceedings to repossess the property would be put on hold.

David put the phone down and wondered what had just happened. Before he'd picked up the phone, he'd thought the only outcome was already set in motion. But it was clear the situation was not as he'd assumed and there could be a way of holding onto their house after all.

The phone on his desk rang and he picked it up. It was Melissa.

"David, I've got Lucy for you. Can I put her through?"

Lucy very rarely called him at work. David's heart immediately pounded in his chest with the thought something bad must have happened.

The phone line clicked, and he heard Lucy's breathing on the other end of the phone.

"David, it's Annabel. She's fallen off her bike on the way to work this morning. She's a bit shaken up though, as some bloke in the park jumped out from behind a bush and frightened her. He said he was the park gardener and was very apologetic. I think it was the same chap who jumped out at me. Apparently, he said he knew you and me and wanted to pass a message on to you. He apologised for jumping out a bit quickly on Annabel. It's all very odd and a bit creepy to be honest David. Anyway, could you pop over to the school in your lunch hour and check she's OK? I'm just on my way out to work myself now. Did you speak to the bank?"

David was wondering what George's message could be and had hardly registered that Annabel may have hurt herself in the fall. "Er yes, I have. Fantastic news – they've agreed that if we pay the full amount each month for the next three months rather than the reduced amount I've been paying, they will pause the repossession proceedings. I told them about the new contract and how it was likely to change our circumstances and they accepted this for now. Looks like we may be able to hold onto the house after all Lucy."

There was a pause and David wondered whether Lucy was still there.

"Lucy?"

"Yes, it's OK David. It's just I've been thinking this morning, perhaps it's time we moved to a smaller house anyway. The girls will eventually move out and we'll be left rattling around in this big house. Maybe we need to move in a new direction David and we just need to go with it."

David laughed. "I was thinking that selling the house or, worse still, losing it completely, could be the end of something wonderful. But thinking about it from a different perspective, perhaps it could be the start of a wonderful new adventure for us too."

"Yes David. I was listening to one of my CDs this morning, from one of the speakers at the 'Be the Best' event, and he was saying life is like a two-sided coin, both with different pictures but both part of the same life and both of equal value. He said we need to flip over the coin to see the other side, simply by looking at our difficulties as opportunities too. It got me thinking that perhaps if we moved, it would ease the financial pressure a little, free up some cash and enable us to live a little. I've even been looking at the holidays in the sun we could afford if we sold the house. We haven't had a proper holiday for nearly 3 years now David. Anyway, I need to let you get back to work. Do pop over and check on Annabel at lunchtime, won't you? See you later, love you."

The phone clicked without David even having the chance to respond. As he placed the receiver back onto its cradle, he let out a small chuckle. The last 24 hours had been a roller coaster of emotions and a real test of his belief systems, and in a strange and unfamiliar way, his faith too; not in some sort of supreme being but in his own ability to manage his way through difficult periods. He realised if he looked at his situations from different perspectives it would either give him hope or despair. One would drain his energy whilst the other would build energy up within him. He decided he wanted to build his energy up rather than drain him towards the darkness despair can create. He was determined to pull out the weeds in his mind before they had chance to take hold.

The rest of the day passed uneventfully, but David's positive mood remained. He popped over to the school at lunchtime as instructed by Lucy. Annabel reassured him she was fine and simply spooked by the park gardener rather than the topple from her bike.

During the afternoon he continued to think of new ideas and ways to help the business grow and their personal finances improve. He left the office with a spring in his step he hadn't felt for some time.

On the way home, he decided to go into the park to find George, firstly to check he was OK after his bump with Annabel, and to find out his message. He wanted to hear it directly from him rather than waiting to hear it from Annabel, who he hadn't wanted to press on the matter when he'd seen her at lunchtime. She would no doubt embellish the story in her own dramatic way anyway.

He pulled the car onto his driveway and then headed towards the park and the usual gated entrance. The robin was back and was tweeting a merry tune as if it too had picked up on the positivity of the day.

David headed through the park towards the cemetery, hoping to find George, but he was nowhere to be seen. After nearly an hour of wandering through parts of the park David had never truly explored, he gave up and began to head towards the exit gate and his home. As he passed a small copse of trees, he could hear wood being cut within the small wooded area. The chainsaw was whining as it cut through trees and David wondered if it was George who was hiding just a few metres away. He decided to head into the wood to see if George was the busy woodcutter and after a few steps into the tress, there he was, busily chopping down trees in what appeared to be quite a random manner.

"Hey George, how are you?"

"Hello boyo. Have you come to give me a right telling off after I scared your girl this morning?" George took off his cap and mopped his brow, sweat glistening in the late evening fading light.

"Annabel's fine George but you did give her a fright. She says you jumped out at her!"

"I don't jump out at anyone boyo. I'm a park gardener so I've no idea why people are surprised to see me. Anyways, she gave you my message then as you've come by here to find me?"

"No, although I saw her briefly at lunchtime to check how she was, I didn't ask her about your message I'm afraid."

"Well that's funny boyo, as my message was for you to meet me here tonight so I could show you the clearing. Well, now you're here, I wanted to show you how when we remove some of the trees, we get more light to the floor. For new things to grow, sometimes we must lose something to create the space and light for new starts. Do you know what I'm saying?"

David thought he knew where George was heading but George could see the puzzled look on David's face.

"You know you've been working hard on your weeding and making sure they don't take hold? Well, sometimes we need to carry out some thinning-out of healthy vegetation to create the light for new things to grow. Sometimes it means taking a chainsaw to things that are fine as they are but are stifling everything else around them."

David was thinking about his house and that maybe letting it go would create space for a new start.

The two men chatted about the wood, the trees George was felling and how it would make the wood healthier, encouraging brand-new plants, insects and animals to investigate. What seemed like brutal and perhaps unnecessary destruction was part of creating something new.

As David began to say his goodbyes and make a move towards his home, George stopped him.

"Just before you go boyo, take this with you." He tossed a coin over to David who caught it with one hand. David turned the coin over and realised it had a head on both sides.

"You see David, if you keep your head, you can't lose." George winked at him.

"Thanks George. I appreciate what you're saying. See you again soon."

"I guarantee it boyo!"

David waved to George and headed back towards the gate exit. The light was fading fast and there was no sign of the robin as David exited the park. As he walked up the road towards his house, David noticed a van was parked on their driveway. On the back it had the name 'Antony Boulton, Your Local Estate Agent' painted across the doors.

By the time David walked up his driveway, the front door was opening and a smartly dressed young man was shaking hands with Lucy. He nearly bumped into David as he turned towards him.

"Sorry sir. You must be Mr Turner, yes?"

"Yes, I'm David Turner."

"Well I'm Peter Seaton-Wright from Antony Boulton Estate Agents. You've certainly got a lovely house Mr Turner and I think you'd have no problem selling it. The market has certainly picked up and prices are rising. I'd love the chance to manage your sale and I've given Mrs Turner an outline of our services and prices. I'll let you get inside Mr Turner and I hope to be hearing from you soon."

David wasn't listening. He stood motionless, looking at the young man standing in front of him who bore an uncanny resemblance to his deceased son.

"Er... yes... OK Peter, thanks for coming over. We'll, er... be in touch I guess..."

"I hope so sir, your house feels very familiar to me. But sometimes it's time to move on, isn't it, Mr Turner? If we hang on to the past too long, new memories can't be created, can they?"

Peter Seaton-Wright walked down the drive to his van, waved and got in. After a few moments, he waved again, reversed off the drive and was gone. David was still standing on the drive looking in the direction Peter had driven.

"Are you thinking what I'm thinking David?" said Lucy, interrupting David's thoughts.

"Well, depends on what you're thinking!" suggested David.

"Did he remind you of our Peter?"

"Yes, he did. It made my blood freeze I can tell you. I've no idea what he said to me to be honest. It was like seeing a ghost of our own son."

"Come on inside David. It's getting cold. I'll tell you all about what he said to me, including a bizarre story about a horse. It was all very surreal."

David followed Lucy into the house and after removing his jacket and shoes, he headed into the kitchen where Lucy was starting to prepare their supper. David sat down at one of the kitchen chairs.

"You decided to speak to some estate agents then Lucy?"

"Well, yes. I've even got quite excited about a new house David. It could be a fresh start for us. We could clear the arrears on the mortgage, maybe move away from all the memories this house holds for us. Not so we forget, but just so we can create some new ones. How was your day anyway? Any more info from the bank? Annabel tells me you popped into see her."

David gave more details of his conversation with the bank and how the financial pressure had been removed, for the time being anyway. He also told Lucy about George and how he'd been clearing trees in the park to encourage new growth. Lucy agreed it sounded like their own lives. However, David was curious about Peter Seaton-Wright and his story.

"Well it was really odd David. I'd rung the estate agent at 11.00am to ask them if they could send someone round to value the property but they said they had no-one available until tomorrow. I said that was fine and then within 10 minutes, Peter turned up at the door. I told him a little of our circumstances and he was very upbeat, telling me that often endings are just beginnings of something new."

"Gosh, that's weird," David said.

"Then he told me a story he said was very ancient. He even pulled out a piece of paper with the story written down, as if he had come prepared to give it to me. Look, this is it."

Lucy handed a slightly crumpled piece of paper with a title at the top which said, 'The Farmer and the Horse'.

"Read it out David. I'd like to hear it again. Then maybe I'll understand why he gave it to me."

David started to read the story.

'One day a farmer's horse ran away. The following day the farmer saw his neighbour and told him his horse had run away. The neighbour was very concerned and told the farmer he was sorry about the loss of his horse. But the farmer replied simply by saying "Who knows what's good or bad?" The neighbour was confused because the loss of the horse was clearly terrible news, being the most valuable

thing he owned. The following day, the horse came back but was accompanied by twelve wild horses which were running around the farmer's field. The neighbour came rushing over to the farmer to celebrate and he congratulated the farmer on his good fortune. The farmer simply replied again: "Who knows what's good or bad?" The very next day the farmer's son was taming one of the wild horses and he was thrown off and broke his leg. On hearing the news, the neighbour comes back once more to say how sorry he was to hear about the terrible news of his son's injury. The farmer repeated again: "Who knows what's good or bad?" The day after the farmer's son had his accident and injured his leg, the army came through the village and conscripted able-bodied young men to go and fight in the war. The son was spared conscription because of his broken leg. The neighbour was convinced the farmer would be delighted his son had been spared but when the neighbour asked him, he simply said...'

David looked up at Lucy. "What did Peter say was the point of the story?"

"He didn't need to explain it David. I understood that whether things are good or bad is simply a matter of perspective. It's simply all about how we look at things."

"You're right Lucy. I've spent the whole day hearing the same message from various people. Even Eric gave me the same message. How weird. I still can't get over how similar he looked to our Peter too. It spooked me to be honest. What did you agree with him then?"

"Nothing really. He said he'd report back to the office and if we're keen to proceed, we should give them a call. What do you think? Should we put the house up for sale?"

David had been thinking about it all day and couldn't think of a compelling reason to stay where they were. Maybe it was time to create a clearing and allow some space for new growth. They talked more but came to no genuine conclusion, so decided to sleep on it.

After a relaxed evening, David slept soundly. So soundly in fact, he slept through the alarm and Lucy needed to wake him up with a nudge and a cup of tea. As David prepared for work, he felt a new wave of hope and faith come over him. He wondered if their lives had turned a corner.

When he came down for breakfast, the girls had already left, and Lucy was getting ready to leave the house too.

"I've left some details on the kitchen table for you to look at. It's about the conference. I'd still like to go. In fact, I feel even more strongly now that we need to go, so I hope you're still up for it."

"Yes of course. I thought we'd already booked the tickets and the hotel?"

Lucy put her hand on his shoulder. "Yes, I know we have but with everything that's happened recently, I wanted to check you still wanted to go."

"Absolutely. I reckon we'll be able to teach these positive mindset gurus a thing or two by the time we get there!"

"OK, if you're sure. I'll see you later. And I'll call the estate agents today and get the process for the house moving forward too."

"Yes, that's fine love. See you later."

Lucy blew David a kiss and then briskly walked down the hall and out of the door. David was left in the silent house with just the hum of the electrical appliances for company. He recalled how a few short weeks ago, he'd sat in silence in the same spot wondering whether his life was even worth living. Many things had changed and yet much remained the same. He still had the business and he was still in the same house with the same family. His financial situation hadn't changed dramatically but his perspective had changed and so had some of the opportunities that now lay before him.

His mobile phone rang and buzzed on the worktop where it was plugged into the wall for its overnight charge. On the screen, he could see it was Lucy who'd only left a few minutes ago. David assumed she'd forgotten something.

"Hello love, are you OK?"

"No David. I'm trembling."

"Oh my God, what's happened? Are you OK?"

"Nothing's happened David, I'm fine but I've just rang the estate agents. I thought I'd catch them before I went into work."

David was puzzled about the sense of urgency in Lucy's voice.

"What's wrong then?"

"There's no one called Peter Seaton-Wright at their branch David and they told me again they couldn't have sent anyone round yesterday anyway. When I told them he was in a van with their logo on the side, they told me they don't have vans and certainly none with logos on. I told them Peter had come round to see us just 10 minutes after I'd spoken to them and they insisted no-one called Peter worked for them. I had to apologise and put the phone down."

David was stunned.

"Are you there David?"

"Yes, I'm here. I'm just taking in what you're saying Lucy. Who the heck was Peter Seaton-Wright then? Did he intercept your call or something and is passing himself off as an estate agent to get our money?"

"But he didn't ask me for money David. He just listened to me and then told me the story about the farmer and the horse. Then you came back. It's all a bit creepy. He looked just like our Peter too..." Lucy's voice faded away as if she couldn't believe what she was saying.

"I know. But whoever he was, his message to us stands. It's all about our perspective. I've met many random people with messages for me in the last few weeks so another stranger giving us a message of hope is fine by me. I'm not going to let this change my perspective Lucy. We've turned a corner and maybe Peter Seaton-Wright was a guardian angel sent to keep us heading in the right direction."

"OK David. As long as you're sure he wasn't some weird stalker or nutcase who's watching us."

David wasn't sure about anything other than he wasn't worried about Peter Seaton-Wright. The feeling was one of reassurance rather than fear, which was the perspective he chose to put on it.

"No, Peter is on our side Lucy. I'm certain of it."

PART
THREE

16.

Over the next few weeks, life continued to improve for David. The contracts the business had won began to materialise, and he'd been busy interviewing and taking on new staff. Billy stepped up and became a willing and very capable member of the team, eventually heading up an extended team of counter staff. Mel worked tirelessly behind the scenes to ensure materials were always available, suppliers paid on time and cashflow managed effectively. And Eric even agreed to a quiet drink in the local pub on his final day and shed a few tears when David presented him with a gold watch, engraved on the back with his name, the letters TJS for Turner Plumbing Supplies and his years' service.

Despite hearing nothing more about Peter Seaton-Wright, and Lucy's protests about using Antony Boulton Estate Agents, the house had gone on the market with them and had attracted a lot of interest, with several potential buyers vying to be first in line to purchase. So much had happened very quickly, David had not spent any time walking through the park and had therefore not enjoyed any further chance meetings with unusual or unexpected characters. Life had seemed to return to some sense of normality, with a routine and rhythm which seemed much more relaxed and easier going than David had experienced for some time. Life felt good again.

The 'Be the Best' conference was now upon them and David had organised his time off work. Mel had reassured him a weekend away was just what he needed and that she would hold the fort, or more likely be on the end of the phone if anything went wrong in the depot, which was now working over the weekend to keep up with deliveries.

Just before he left the office for the weekend of the conference, David called Mel into his office for a final debrief.

"Are you sure you'll be OK manning the phone over the weekend Mel?"

"Yes David. It's as if you don't trust me to cope, which after all these years is a little frustrating." Mel had a look on her face to suggest she was already tired of the conversation and turned to leave the office.

"Mel, just before you go. Can I ask you something?"

Mel turned back towards David. "Of course."

"Why do you think our fortunes have changed around Mel? How can things be going well when for so long it looked like the business wasn't going to survive?" David's voice cracked as he finished his sentence. "I need to keep pinching myself."

Mel sat down on the chair opposite David's desk.

"You're a good man who was going through a tough time David. Most of us endure periods in our life when nothing seems to make sense. Maybe that's when we should look to something bigger than ourselves for help. You survived a mild heart attack and maybe it was the wake-up call you needed to change your life and perhaps it changed your perspective too. You also listened to people around you and accepted help, when before you thought you could solve all your problems yourself. None of us are existing in this life alone David and we all need some help and guidance from time to time. Perhaps this was your time to receive that advice and support. All I know is that your perspective on life and business has changed. As a result, your life and business has changed too. It thrills me David to see you looking well too. Go and enjoy your weekend amongst all those positive people. I'm sure you'll give them all a run for their money!"

Mel got up from the chair and David sat for a few more moments thinking about all the people he'd met and the messages they'd given him, right from the first walk in the park when he'd met Michael. He wondered if he'd ever see him again, or perhaps he'd just appeared when he'd needed someone to talk to.

He picked up his briefcase, grabbed his jacket, flicked off the light switch in the office and headed for the door. He could see Billy still behind the counter in the depot scrutinising something on the computer screen in front of him. All the other lights had been turned off and there were no other staff left and yet Billy was still transfixed by something on his screen.

"Everything OK Billy? Don't you have a home to go to?"

Billy looked up. "Hi boss, I didn't know you were still here. I'm just answering an email which came in just before I was heading home. It's puzzled me a bit so I'm wondering how to respond to it."

"Is it a complaint Billy? Can I help at all?"

"No boss. It's just the opposite. It's from a guy who's just signed off as Michael. He didn't even provide a surname. He's said some very nice things about me. He must've come into the branch some time, but I don't remember serving him."

"Did you say Michael?" David was already walking over to the counter where Billy stood motionless. "What does the email say?"

"That's the strange thing. He's complimenting me on the way I've helped you. He says sometimes people need to be ready to accept help and that he told you this a while ago when you first met him. He says that I've been part of the help and he's noticed. Then he simply said to pass on a message to you. I'm to tell you you're ready to set some new goals now. He then signed off with his name. I've been standing here wondering who he is and what his email means for the last twenty minutes. I'll turn off the computer now, as I think it's time to go home. Why are you smiling boss?"

David wasn't just smiling; he was grinning and ready to laugh. He'd just been wondering if he'd ever see Michael again and then he turns up on Billy's email. He remembered Michael had told him in their very first conversation that he had to be ready to accept help and that Mel had just been saying this to him too. He also recalled one of Michael's first questions to him was about goals and dreams. His mindset then had been to dismiss Michael as a cranky old man who had got lost from a local old people's home. But that conversation has since sparked a series of unexplained encounters which now find him preparing to go off with Lucy on a weekend conference with motivational speakers, workshops and seminars all about being your best and more than likely, about setting new goals for his life and business.

"Don't worry Billy. Just delete the email. I think I know who Michael is. He's a good friend I met a while ago. You get off home now and just before you go, I'd like to thank you for all your hard work and commitment. It's a genuine pleasure having you working with us."

"That's good of you to say Mr Turner. I love working here and helping others. Every time I help someone with their problems, it makes me feel good. To spend all day helping people is about the best job I could have. Thank you for giving me the chance."

As Billy shut down his computer and headed for the door, he didn't tell David he hadn't quite told the truth about

Michael. He did know who he was as he'd been into the branch a few times and had spoken to Billy but had asked him not to mention to David he'd seen him. Initially, he thought he was a bit strange, but he'd offered Billy advice on how to view his opportunity at Turner Plumbing Supplies. Billy had found the man oddly engaging, and he only ever came into the depot when no-one else was around. Billy had begun to look forward to seeing him, but every time he left, he got Billy to promise he wouldn't tell David about his visits. When David was in hospital with his heart attack, Michael was in David's office talking to Mel, but she'd never mentioned Michael to him, so he'd never mentioned Michael to Mel.

Billy pulled the door shut and headed for his bus stop which was just outside the branch. David was pulling out of the car park and he waved to Billy who waved back, wondering exactly who Michael was.

17.

When David pulled the car onto the drive in front of his house, he noticed the word 'Sold' had been put against the For Sale sign in the front garden. Lucy had texted him at 3pm to say the offer they had accepted for their house was confirmed and the house was therefore 'Sold – Subject to Contract.'

As he put his key in the door, it opened, and Lucy was standing in front of him with a huge smile. "We've done it then. No turning back now!"

She threw her arms around his neck and hugged him even before he'd had a chance to put down his briefcase.

"Blimey Lucy! I thought part of you might be sad it was sold so quickly?"

Lucy let go of her vice-like grip and David put down his briefcase, following Lucy as she headed for the kitchen.

"I thought I would feel sad. After all, we've had our children while we've been here and yes, this house is full of memories. But a lovely young couple came round today to see the house and I managed to get time out of work to meet them. They reminded me of us when we moved in. They want a family and to start a new life here. I thought about the story of the farmer and the horse that Peter Seaton-Wright gave me and realised this is all about how we look at things. I could see that whilst it would be an ending for us, it was the beginning for them. When I had a call from the estate agent with their offer, I accepted it."

"How much did they offer then?"

"The full asking price! They said they just felt the house was right for them and I felt they were the right people to pass on our house to, so I accepted their offer. The estate agent was here within an hour putting the Sold sign up. It was a real whirlwind. Did I do the right thing David?"

"Definitely. Maybe it was just meant to be that this first couple to view the house were the right people. With all that's happened recently, I'm not at all surprised by anything!"

"I know," said Lucy. "I was also reading something in the brochure for the conference and this man was talking about our belief system and how it either gives us energy or it takes it from us, but we have a choice on how we look at things. Whilst I'm sad to let go of this house, I'm choosing to see this as a beginning and not an end. And I think it's perfect timing for our trip to the conference don't you think?"

David sat down at the kitchen table where many conversations had taken place over the years. Part of him felt sad too but he could sense something else within him too. It was hope for a better future that had perhaps already begun.

"Come on love," said Lucy. "We need to get cracking if we are going to get the train tonight up to Birmingham. I've got the suitcases all sorted and here are our tickets. You go and freshen up a little. I've put the clothes you chose this morning on the bed. We need to be out of here by about 4.30pm if we are going to get to Euston in time for our train."

David took a deep breath, got up from the chair and kissed Lucy on the check. "I love you Lucy."

"Ah, you soppy so and so. Get on up those stairs. We've got a conference to go to!"

David bounded up the stairs, quickly got undressed and jumped in the shower. He dried quickly and put on the clothes Lucy had laid out on their bed for him. Within 10 minutes, he was back downstairs where Lucy was waiting for him in the hall.

"I think that's a record David. Come on then, let's go. I've left a note for the girls and we can ring them when we get to the hotel."

David picked up the suitcase Lucy had packed and knew everything he needed would be in the case. They'd gone through everything together before David had left in the morning and as they pulled the door too behind them, David caught sight of a figure at the bottom of the road. He was waving frantically in their direction. As they walked down the road towards Highgate tube station just a few minutes from their home, the man was hurriedly heading towards them. As the figure got closer, David recognised him. It was George the park gardener.

"Hey boyo! Wait up will you!"

Lucy grabbed David's arm and pulled him to a halt. "That's the chap who jumped out on me and bumped into Annabel on her bike. I've no idea why he's here or how he's found us."

As George came towards them, he was clearly out of breath and sweating heavily from the exertion of walking up the road from the park.

"David and Lucy. I'm glad I've found you before you've left. I wanted to give you a message a while back, but I haven't seen you in the park. You see, I was weeding some beds this afternoon and I was having real trouble getting some of the little blighters to move and you popped into my head again and I knew my message was even more impor-tant. So, I raced up here to see you. Phew! An old man like me is in no right condition to rush about. Look at me. Where are my manners?" George thrust out his dirty, soil covered hand towards Lucy. "Nice to meet you again Lucy."

"Hello George. You must be more careful when you're in the park. You knocked our daughter off her bike!"

"I know Mrs Turner, I'm really sorry that happened. I'm a bit clumsy me you see. Anyways, I know you're going up to Birmingham today, so let me tell you what I need to tell you."

"How do you know we're going to Birmingham? Who told you?" Lucy asked.

David didn't need to know how George knew. But he did need to know what message he had for them. "What's up George? What do we need to know?"

"Well, it's about the weeds you see. They often grow most where good plants grow and now you've planted seeds in good soil, you'll come across more weeds that try to choke you up David. You see, them that tries to stop good things happening will be hard at work to stop you and Miss Lucy here getting to Birmingham. The closer you get to good things, the harder they work to stop you. It's normal but just keep going David."

Lucy squeezed David's arm, clearly spooked by George's sudden appearance and strange advice.

"What do you mean George?" said David. "And who are you talking about?"

"You don't need to know David. They be in the shadows y'see. Just don't let them stop you."

Lucy was pulling David away from George and the strange conversation. "Can we go please David. We're going to miss our train."

"It's OK Lucy my lovely," said George. "I know I be a bit of a strange sort rushing up to you and telling you to watch out. But it's my job y'see Lucy. I must pass the message on to David here."

"OK George," said David. "Thanks for the heads up. I'll keep a look out."

"You make sure you do David. Just keep your eyes on this weekend and you'll be right."

"OK George. You take care and thanks for the message. See you soon." David started to move away, and George lifted his cap as they passed. "Safe trip Mrs Turner. Lovely to meet you again."

"Er yes, you too George," Lucy mumbled.

As they walked away, David looked back to wave at George, but he'd gone, clearly keen to get back to his gardening duties in the park.

"What was all that about?" said Lucy. "He was proper weird. Gave me the creeps."

"He's no harm Lucy and don't worry about what he said."

"Yes, but he was suggesting we must look out for people out to stop us. And something about living in the shadows. That's horrible David. Why would he say something like that? I'm a bit frightened now."

David was less unnerved by George's message but knew the fact he'd made so much effort to warn them was important.

As they arrived at Highgate tube station, David found himself more edgy than usual and he scanned the concourse as they entered. There appeared to be long queues at the ticket machines, and he could hear raised voices. The station was much busier than normal, and nobody appeared to be going through the barriers onwards to the platform. The tannoy crackled into life and a voice boomed out over their heads.

"Please leave the station by the nearest exit. The station has been closed temporarily and we would appreciate your cooperation by leaving the station quietly and calmly. There is no need to be alarmed."

Above the voices on the concourse, David heard a distant sound of police sirens and Lucy squeezed his hand.

"Come on Lucy, let's get a cab," and he pulled her out of the station concourse towards the fading daylight.

Outside the station was a more chaotic scene, as angry passengers spilled out onto the street. The sound of sirens was getting louder and David pulled Lucy at a brisker pace towards the main road. A black cab swung around the corner and David stuck out his arm and waved the taxi down. The driver quickly pulled over and David grabbed the door handle, bundled in their suitcase and pushed Lucy in before him.

"Euston station please mate," said David "and make it snappy. We've got a train to catch."

The driver, a Portuguese-looking man, glanced into his rear-view mirror towards David.

"Hello sir, welcome to my taxi. My name is Miguel. Do not worry. I will get you to station safely. London shutdown. Bombs scare, people and roads are blocked everywhere."

David recalled what George had said but dismissed the idea the bomb scares were about him and Lucy.

"Just get us as close as you can to Euston, and then we can walk the final bit."

Lucy was strangely quiet and hadn't said a word since they'd got into the taxi.

"Maybe we should just go home and forget about going to Birmingham. I'm not sure I want to go now anyway after what your gardener friend said."

David squeezed Lucy's hand. "We're going love, even if we have to walk there."

"Do not worry nice lady. Miguel keep you safe. My job to protect you from danger, you have important journey. Miguel taxi will find way."

Miguel took them through various back streets and one-way systems, constantly tutting to himself as he encountered queues of stationary traffic. He kept looking in his rear-view mirror at David who was getting more nervous with each twist and turn.

"You will get to station sir, don't worry!" said Miguel. "My taxi safe for you."

David looked at Lucy who whispered to him, "Why is he so keen to help us?"

"I will do my job lady, no need to worry."

David squeezed Lucy's hand once more and smiled. David felt safe, protected and certain they would reach Euston in time for their train. They sat in silence as Miguel continued to turn and weave his way through the traffic as sirens filled the air. As the taxi approached Euston station, a fire engine sped past in the other direction.

Miguel pulled the taxi to a halt at the underground taxi rank and got out to open the rear door for Lucy. David got out, pulling the suitcase with him and walked around to join Lucy. As he did, in the corner of his eye he caught sight of a flash of red. Miguel was wearing red socks.

"Thanks for getting us here quickly and safely Miguel."

Miguel reached out his hands to shake David's hand. "My pleasure David. See you soon." He then turned and was back in his taxi before David had the chance to respond.

"Are you coming love?" asked Lucy, waiting for David to turn back from watching the taxi disappear around the corner.

David was watching and wondering about Miguel. He'd mentioned his name and said he'd see him soon, which didn't seem to be a throwaway comment. It was if Miguel genuinely meant it. David smiled, remembered his red socks and knew he would indeed see Miguel again.

"Come on David, we'll miss our train!" Lucy was standing with her hands on her hips waiting a few metres away from David. "Why are you looking so happy?"

David walked towards Lucy and smiled. "Because I know we're safe honey and nothing is going to stop us getting to Birmingham."

Lucy looked puzzled. "You're sounding a bit like the freaky gardener bloke."

David put his arm around Lucy and began to walk her toward the concourse at Euston station, pulling the suitcase behind him. "Don't worry about a thing Lucy. This is going to be an awesome weekend."

As they entered the station concourse, it was full of people moving in all sorts of directions. It was clear the mainline routes were running but that the underground station was closed. This meant the concourse was even more full than usual, with people hanging around waiting for instructions from staff who looked harassed and overwhelmed.

A quick glance at the departure board showed David their train was leaving from platform 7 and it was on time. He ushered Lucy across the concourse towards platform 7 and they headed down the short slope towards the train. As they approached the train, all tickets were being inspected by a member of the rail network staff. It was a train run by Virgin Railways and the member of staff was young, female and about 1.5m high. Her uniform appeared to be about three sizes too big and every passenger seemed to tower above her. As they got closer to her, the passenger in front of them appeared to be arguing with her and was gesticulating and shouting.

David and Lucy paused behind the angry looking man who clearly had not got the right ticket to travel on the train.

"Please sir, would you calm down and let me explain what you need to do," said the small and fragile looking member of staff.

The angry passenger seemed even more agitated. "I'm not interested in what you've got to say. I bought a ticket so I'm getting on this train, unless you think you can stop me!"

David instinctively wanted to protect the young member of staff, who was probably no older than Georgia.

"Hey mate, calm down a bit. She's only trying to help!"

The man swung round towards David and towered over him too. "And what's it got to do with you?" He poked David in the chest with his index finger. "Stay out of this mate as it's nowt to do with you."

David was unperturbed by the man's angry demeanour. But Lucy was pulling at David's arm, pleading with him to step back from what was rapidly becoming an ugly scene.

"No mate, you listen. If you've got the wrong ticket, you've got the wrong ticket. Right now, you're stopping all the folks who've got the right tickets from getting on the train. Kindly step aside and allow this young lady to do her job."

The man seemed taken aback by David's calm but direct instructions and for a moment, he paused. "But I need to be on this train," he said, far more calmly than he had before.

The young lady also seemed calmer. "Then please go to the ticket office and exchange your ticket, as I've already explained to you." She turned to David and Lucy and took the tickets Lucy was holding in her hand. "Thank you, madam, that's fine and thank you sir for your willingness to step into a situation over which you had no control. Have a good trip."

David and Lucy walked towards the train. Lucy squeezed David's hand. "My hero," she said. "I can't believe how strong and assertive you were. That man was angry, and he could've pulled a knife or anything."

"No, he was just angry Lucy and I wasn't going to let him stop us getting on the train."

They arrived at their carriage, boarded the train and Lucy headed for the seats she'd booked for them. David left the suitcase in the luggage area and joined her. Within a few minutes the train was moving out of the station towards Birmingham.

David turned to Lucy. "You see love, nothing could stop us getting on this train."

The train picked up speed and was soon away from London and speeding through open countryside. Lucy and David sat in silence for a while and Lucy leant her head against David's shoulder. Within a few more minutes, she'd fallen asleep.

David meanwhile was talking to the silence.

"Who tried to stop us?" he asked, using the voice in his head.

"The shadows," was the response

"But what are the shadows?" he asked himself.

There was no reply.

After an uneventful journey, the train pulled into Birmingham International station. David and Lucy disembarked and headed for the taxi rank just outside the station. A line of four black cabs was waiting and as they approached the first an Asian man stepped out from his cab and slid open the side door for them.

David and Lucy clambered in and David placed the suitcase on the floor in front of them.

"The Crowne Plaza please," said David and the driver nodded and began to drive away from the station.

The radio was on in the taxi and although David and Lucy couldn't hear what was being said, they knew a conversation was taking place about what had been happening in London as they left. David decided to ask the driver if he'd heard anything on the news.

"Do you know what's been happening in London?"

"Yeah, it's all been a load of hoaxes mate. Four tube stations were shut down 'cos they thought there was bombs there. But it's all been a big wind-up mate. Nothing in it. Just trying to cause havoc. Wasters."

The taxi pulled up in front of the hotel and David paid the fare and took the change, placing it in his pocket. They headed over towards the hotel and checked in. Soon, they were in their room. Lucy collapsed onto the bed and threw back her arms.

David was still standing and was looking at something in his hand.

"Are you OK love?" she asked.

David was sorting the coins in his hands. One of the coins wasn't a coin at all. It was a medal, just like the others he'd had with Hope, Faith and Love inscribed on them. But this one had 'Strength' inscribed on one side with the same angel on the other.

"The taxi driver must've given me this in my change," he said.

He showed the coin to Lucy. "Are you sure you didn't have this already?"

"No, I've never had a medal like this one with the word Strength on it. But somehow, it describes today for me perfectly. I've felt strong all day. I knew we were going to be safe in London, that we were going to get the train OK and that the angry man in the station wasn't going to stop us either. It's like I was on some sort of strength drug, giving me calmness and certainty in equal measure. It was almost as if we were being protected today."

Lucy laughed. "Blimey David, I never thought I'd see the day when you'd be talking about strength, protection and guardian angels. But if you think that's the case for today then I'm happy to believe you honey."

After unpacking their clothes, and taking a shower, they headed down into the hotel to find some dinner in the restaurant. Lucy was hoping to bump into some of the people who were attending the 'Be the Best' event, so she could begin to soak up some of the atmosphere. David was more concerned with getting some decent food, followed by a good night's sleep.

As they entered the restaurant, it was already busy, and they were soon shown to a table for two overlooking the grounds of the hotel. The sun had already long disappeared, and it was dark outside with Spring still some way off.

Lucy and David ordered their food and a bottle of red wine which arrived after a short wait, along with a white card which the waiter explained had been given to him by an old man at the bar, with strict instructions it was to be given to David.

The card was blank on one side and on the other were the words, 'Delighted you arrived safely. And remember, strength is always given to the one who needs it most. Your good friend. Michael'.

David looked around the bar area but couldn't see anyone who looked like Michael.

"What does the card say David?"

David folded the card in two and placed it under his side plate on the table in front of him. "It was just a note to welcome us to the hotel Lucy. A nice touch actually."

"Ah that's lovely. I'm looking forward to tomorrow David and I can't quite believe we're here after the last few crazy weeks. It's just a few short weeks ago that the business was struggling and there looked like there was no way out. Then you have a heart attack, the business takes an incredible turn, we sell the house and you agree to come along to this conference. I can't believe how things can change so quickly. I wonder if the speakers tomorrow can match what we've been through recently!"

"I know Lucy. It's been an incredible journey. But it feels like it's just beginning. Let's drink to a new and brighter future."

They clinked their glasses together and toasted a new beginning. David wondered if it was a new beginning or the ending of something. Or if in fact, that was the same thing.

They enjoyed their meal, with easy chatter about the girls, work and the house move. The evening was as relaxed a time as David could recall and they even began to chat about what the conference might bring for them. David noticed how Lucy sparkled as she talked about the day ahead and he delighted in sharing her excitement. Just a few weeks ago, he was in a hospital bed, not knowing what the future held, and now he was about to do something he'd never done. It felt exhilarating.

They headed to their room after their meal and eased into the most contented and deep sleep David had experienced in many years.

18.

The alarm on David's phone woke them up with a start at 7.00am. They'd agreed to take breakfast at 8.00am and to be ready to leave for the short walk to the conference centre by 8.45am. Registration opened at 9.00am and Lucy had planned the morning very carefully. She didn't want to be late.

Once they'd showered and dressed, they headed down to breakfast and in David's case, enjoyed a full English breakfast. Lucy was too excited and nervous to eat much. Lucy was curious to see if any other guests were heading for the conference, but it was impossible to spot. David ticked her off for listening in to the conversations of others around the restaurant to see if she could spot other delegates.

They returned to their room and after some tooth brushing and final adjustments to their smart casual attire, they were ready.

"I can't quite believe this is happening David," said Lucy as they stood just about to open their bedroom door. "I had a dream one day we'd do something like this together and here we are about to share an experience that could change our lives forever."

David pulled Lucy to him and held her tightly. "I think our lives are already changed forever Lucy."

David opened the bedroom door and they headed down to the lobby of the hotel and out onto the hotel concourse. The sun was shining and as they headed towards the conference centre, just a short walk away, they could hear music getting louder. The numbers of people heading towards the conference was growing as more people joined from nearby car parks, and as they got even closer, still more alighted from buses and headed excitedly towards the venue.

As they approached the conference centre, the music became more recognisable and was clearly designed to generate enthusiasm and excitement. Lucy squeezed David's hand and he knew she was feeling the apprehension and increase in adrenalin everything about the event was choreographed to do.

David, however, felt the cynic in him whispering at the edge of his consciousness. Like weeds creeping into his senses, the positivity of the previous few days was being replaced with a more familiar and altogether more comfortable feeling he recognised. "It's all just designed to make you part with more of your hard-earned cash," he thought.

As they entered the lobby of the conference centre, they could see through two sets of double doors that the hall was huge, with chairs lined up in rows and a stage lit up with flashing lights, images of the speakers being thrown up onto large screens.

They headed for the registration desk where a small queue was forming to get their passes for the weekend. As they arrived at the queue, David felt a slap on his shoulder.

"David Turner, if I live and breathe. I never thought I'd see you at an event like this! You're the original cynic!"

"Gosh, hello Bob. How are you, we've not seen each other in about 10 years! This is my wife Lucy. Lucy, this is Bob Francis. We went to school together, but I've not seen Bob since we met up at the tools' exhibition in London. How's it going Bob and what on earth brings you here?"

"I could ask you the same question me old mucker, but I've been coming along to conferences like these for years. I love 'em. Gives me a real boost and keeps me on my toes I can tell you. There's no complacency allowed here mate, so I hope you're ready to have your head blown off today!"

David was thinking that it was exactly this sort of blind enthusiasm the conference organisers loved. The cynic within him was growing with every second.

"I'm sure you're right Bob," said David, mustering up as much enthusiasm as he could.

"And you Lucy, what brings you along to an event like this?"

Lucy blushed. "Well, I just like being positive and after what we've been through over the past few months, I am hoping this will give us both a new perspective."

"Wow Dave, you need to keep hold of this one. She's got her head screwed on tight mate!"

Bob's brand of brash enthusiasm was now beginning to grate on David, and he looked along the queue to see how far from the registration desk they were, hoping this would give him an excuse to say cheerio to cheery Bob.

"Yep Bob, Lucy is a diamond."

"What you doing now Dave? Still living in your old man's shadow at that plumbing business or have you branched out on yer own?"

"My dad passed away a few years ago Bob, so I took over the business and we're doing fine thanks." David could feel his irritation rising and Lucy picked up on his discomfort.

"What do you do Bob?" asked Lucy.

"Run me own little training business. Chucked in the corporate career at Sharps Tools and decided to start a training company. Tough for the first few years until I met a coach who put me right. Changed my whole philosophy. Awesome guy called Michael and he got me thinking completely different about my business. Bumped into him at a conference like this about four years ago and I ain't looked back since."

David's ears pricked up at the sound of Michael's name once again, as they shuffled forwards in the queue.

"What did this coach bloke tell you then that was so profound?"

"Well that's the weird thing you see. I was only chatting to him for about ten minutes, but he told me I was looking in the wrong place for success. I'd written down my goals and put dream boards together, with pictures on and stuff, but he told me I was looking in the wrong place for my dreams. He told me I had to start with finding my purpose. So, I did and I ain't looked back since."

David was now fully engaged listening to Bob. The cynic voice was backing away as curiosity was now taking over.

"What did this bloke Michael look like Bob?"

"Look like? Well, I can't say I recall really. He was just casually dressed in jeans and a shirt I think, nothing special. Oh, other than I do remember one thing. He had these crazy bright red socks on. You couldn't miss 'em. Proper bright they were, like a scarlet colour. I remember them alright!"

"Are you alright David?" said Lucy, slightly worried about David who'd gone very quiet.

"Er... yes. I'm fine Lucy. Just thinking about what Bob was saying."

"Anyway, I'd better be getting inside as I'm one of Anton's team today, so I need to go and find out me duties. I hope you enjoy the weekend and if I see you in the bar later, I'll let you buy me a drink Dave." Bob slapped David on the shoulder again and laughed.

"Yeah, cheers Bob. Have a good conference."

Bob was walking away when he suddenly turned back towards David and Lucy.

"One other thing the bloke Michael told me. He said I should talk to the silence in between me thoughts. Been doing it ever since and it's never let me down! See ya!"

Lucy turned to David. "What was he on about? Silence between your thoughts? Sounds freaky to me. He's a bit full on, isn't he?"

David knew exactly what Bob was talking about, but it would've meant talking to Lucy about Michael, and he wasn't ready to do that yet.

"I'm not sure to be honest love, but I can tell you he's a changed man. When I last met Bob, he was fed up with his job, quiet and withdrawn. Now he looks like he's taken an overdose of positivity pills!"

"Hello sir, your names please." It was one of the girls on the registration desk and it was clearly David and Lucy's turn to pick up their badges.

"David and Lucy Turner please," said David.

"Yes, your badges are here. Would you like to purchase a programme of events over the next two days? It gives you all the background on the speakers and a little more about how you can work with them after the event. The programme is just five pounds."

"Yes please," said Lucy, reaching into her bag to find her purse to pay for the programme.

They clipped the badges to their clothes and headed towards the main arena. Lucy was flipping through the pages of the programme as she walked, while David was beginning to feel more and more agitated about the whole thing and was wondering why he'd agreed to come. An arena full of a thousand overly enthusiastic people was not his idea of fun.

"Be careful about the weeds that grow in your garden," said a voice from just behind David. He swung round expecting to see George the park gardener behind him. But there was no one who looked even remotely like a gardener.

David continued to follow Lucy towards their allocated seats, which were on the side of the arena with the stage on their right. They were halfway up and in the middle of a row, which meant having to ask other people to stand up to let them pass. Eventually, they found their seats and David sat down, letting out a gasp of frustrated and dejected air.

Lucy was looking around her excitedly and David felt a pang of guilt for not sharing her enthusiasm for what lay ahead. She started talking to the person sitting next to her and they were soon exchanging names and reasons for attending the conference.

David decided to try to access the silence between his thoughts to try to get some of his own advice. He closed his eyes and a memory of Samuel Hutchinson came into his mind. He could see Samuel looking up at the stained-glass window in the chapel where they'd said the Lord's Prayer together. As he recalled the memory, the silence spoke to him.

"Have faith."

David opened his eyes quickly and Lucy was tapping his arm.

"Where had you gone love? Looked like you were away with the fairies!"

David smiled. "I was just gathering my thoughts together honey. Who's on first?"

"The first speakers are like a warmup act, I think. They're going to explain how the conference will run and when the breaks will be etc and then the first main speaker of the day will be on."

"When is your man Anton on then?"

"Not until tomorrow afternoon love. He's the main speaker and will close the event. I'm looking forward to hearing him."

Keep your purse in your bag then love, thought David.

"Have faith," responded the voice inside David's head once more.

A slightly overweight lady was trying to get comfortable in the seat next to David and she appeared hot and flustered. "Sorry my dear. These seats are never big enough for my big lump I'm afraid."

"That's fine. I'm David, and this is my wife Lucy."

The lady leant over in front of David to shake Lucy's hand and David caught a whiff of body odour. It reminded him of Mary, the vagrant he'd met in the park.

"Have faith," the voice inside his head repeated once more.

"I'm Mary and this is my husband George." She reached out her hand and shook David's hand.

The microphones crackled on stage. "Ladies and gentlemen, please take your seats. Be the Best will commence in five minutes!"

David cringed. The voice had an American accent.

As Mary shuffled uncomfortably in her seat, from the corner of his eye, David noticed that George reminded him of the park gardener. He wore a blue and white checked shirt and had a flat cap on his head. He looked completely out of place from those around him.

"What brings you here then?" said Mary, looking from David to Lucy.

Lucy spoke first. "I work for Langham Solicitors and David runs a plumbing merchants' business. We've come to get some positive input and ideas, as we're making some big changes in our lives. How about you?"

"Well, we've come to play our part as and when needed. Sometimes it's what you give that matters, isn't it?"

Lucy was puzzled by Mary's reply, while David was still thinking about Mary the vagrant and George the park gardener. "Where are you from?" he asked.

"Oh, here and there, wherever we need to be to get the work done."

The microphone crackled once more. "Ladies and gentlemen, please take your seats, the conference will begin in two minutes."

The noise in the conference hall started to increase, with a sense of excitement and anticipation. David, however, was feeling more and more uncomfortable and was struggling with the odour coming off the lady squeezed into the seat next to him.

Mary leant towards him and the smell grew stronger, almost burning his nostrils. She turned to look straight into his eyes.

"Don't be too quick to judge my friend. Everything may not be as it seems. Sometimes our greatest gifts come to us when we least expect it."

David caught a flash of red in the corner of his eye. He turned towards George who was wiping his brow with a bright red handkerchief. George looked at David, replaced his cap on his head and stuffed his handkerchief in his trouser pocket. He leant across Mary and spoke to David.

"You see David, there's always a bigger plan but you just can't see it. It's like in your garden. There are things growing underneath the soil that you can't see. You don't need to see them to know they're there. You gotta have faith you see, in the bigger plan."

Lucy nudged David and leant towards him. "What's he on about love?" she whispered.

"God knows," said David.

"Yep, he does," whispered Mary in his ear.

The conference hall lights began to dim, and music started to play, booming across the arena. Lights from the stage started to flash and beam across the room, creating a blaze of colours as images flashed on three big screens erected at the centre and either side of the stage.

Everyone stood up and started clapping and David found himself rising to his feet alongside Lucy. He looked around and people were shouting and whistling in an excitable, disturbing frenzy. It felt like a religious cult to David, with everyone thinking and feeling the same thing.

"Ladies and gentlemen, will you please welcome to the stage, your hosts for 'Be the Best,' Felicity and Paul Stokes!"

Dry ice bellowed across the stage, creating a mist across the arena. Two spotlights appeared at either side of the stage as the two people entered from the left and right side of the stage. As they reached the centre of the stage, they took each other's hands, held them aloft and waved towards the crowd. It reminded David of a US presidential rally, where the candidate would be with their partner, showing the crowd the 'togetherness' of their united approach. The crowd continued to clap, whistle and shout out and David found himself applauding too. He wondered why he was applauding someone he didn't know for a reason yet unclear. But the crowd effect and British courtesy ensured he applauded along with everyone else.

He looked across at Lucy whose face was glowing with excitement. David smiled. This was clearly important to her and he felt a sense of pride that she'd pushed hard for them to be at the conference.

"Please take your seats. Thank you, thank you." Paul Stokes gesticulated for the crowd to sit down while Felicity continued to speak. "You're very kind, thank you. Do take your seats."

The music began to ease off a little and the lights that had been flashing and moving all around the arena began to calm their movements. People started to sit down, and David and Lucy sat down too.

In the excitement of the welcome for the hosts, David hadn't noticed that the two seats next to him were now empty. Mary and George were gone.

19.

Felicity and Paul Stokes were clearly accomplished speakers and appeared to be well-known to many of the delegates at the conference. They explained they were part of the UK Speakers Association and were honoured to be hosting the event on behalf of Robin Anton. They outlined the agenda for both days, talked about fire safety and what to do if an evacuation of the building was required, and then announced each of the speakers. Every speaker's name was met with cheers and applause from the crowd and David joined in too.

"So, do you want to be the best?" cried Paul from the stage.

The crowd roared.

"I didn't hear you!" shouted Felicity. "I said, do you want to be the best?"

The crowd roared even louder.

David looked around the arena, lit up with moving lights and the mist of dry ice. People were clapping and laughing, some were standing up punching the air whilst others sat calmly watching the proceedings unfold. He wondered how many people were there, like him, to support an enthusiastic partner.

Paul and Felicity Stokes told the expectant crowd a little about their own journey through life and work, including a redundancy which led them to start their own business. Certain parts of their story drew gasps, cheers and applause from the crowd and eventually they were ready to introduce the first speaker.

For most of their talk, David was thinking about Mary and George, and wondering why they had mysteriously disappeared. Whilst he was relieved the sickly odour which seemed to follow Mary around had gone, he was disappointed he wasn't able to ask them some of the questions whirring around in his head.

Suddenly, everyone was on their feet cheering and clapping again as the first speaker came onto the stage amidst a blaze of flashing lights, loud music and even more dry ice. His name was Chris Harrison and he told the audience about his life, which clearly had begun in a tough way when he lost his father at a young age. He talked about resilience and determination and his talk ended when his young son, who Chris had indicated was eight years old, came onto the stage and spoke briefly about the importance of not giving up. It was a moving and poignant end to an inspiring talk. However, David remained sceptical, as at the very end of Chris's talk, he outlined how people in the room could work with him. He proceeded to offer discounts and special offers should anyone in the audience wish to sign up for his Personal Development Course (or 'PDC' as he referred to) at the back of the hall. He also indicated that in the foyer was a team of people who would gladly help any delegates. Yes, I'm sure they would be very helpful in getting you to part with your cash, thought David.

The next speaker was a lady called Fiona Sampson, who'd built an online cosmetics business from scratch, based in her own home. Whilst her story was once again inspiring, it too ended with a sales pitch for her own products, including a book she'd written about her life story.

David was finding it hard to keep his sceptical inner voice in check, as the day was already turning out exactly as he expected; a pitch fest for a bunch of speakers delivered to an expectant and easily manipulated audience.

When the first break in proceedings occurred and the audience began to file out of the arena to catch some refreshments and use the toilets, Lucy grabbed David's arm.

"Isn't this brilliant?" she said gleefully. "I loved Fiona, she was so inspirational, wasn't she?"

David was struggling to shake off his scepticism but wanted to be positive for Lucy.

"Yes, it's great," was as much as he could muster.

They entered the lobby of the conference hall, which was buzzing with people and lined with trade stands for the various speakers, along with other businesses wanting to sell their goods and services to the willing crowd.

They lined up in a queue and waited in front of a kiosk offering tea and coffee.

"Well, what do you think then David?" said Lucy.

"It's great love, really good."

"You don't mean that David. I know you. What's the matter, and by the way, where did Mary and George go? Have they gone back to the hotel?"

David realised he could avoid answering Lucy's first question by addressing the second. "I'm not sure love, they must've left not long after it started. They were a strange couple, weren't they?"

"Yes, they were David. George reminded me of the chap with met in the park. His name was George too wasn't it? Very weird."

Lucy chatted to other people in the queue and David made small talk too. Soon, they had their coffees and headed back into the arena where everyone was regathering in anticipation of the next two speakers before lunch.

They were introduced by Felicity and Paul with consistent amounts of dry ice and loud music and delivered their talks and sales pitches, just like the first two speakers. David found his thoughts drifting away from the speakers' messages, which were more of the same: life stories, over-coming challenges and huge successes, followed up by a sales pitch at the end. David found himself thinking about the events of the past few weeks and all the people he'd met and some of the messages he'd taken on board from them.

He thought about Michael; the red envelopes appearing through his letterbox; the medals that seemed to change even whilst he had them in his pockets; his meetings with Samuel Hutchinson and his reconnection to his faith;; the conversations with young salesman John Benjamin and how he'd helped his business; his chats with Tony in hospital along with the strange visit from a tea lady who didn't appear to exist; the milkman who had delivered milk next door for the first time in years; and the messages from George and Mary in their various guises.

David wondered if angels did indeed exist and had tried to help him. He thought about Mel and how she'd trans-formed the business and even Billy who was flourishing. As David pondered all that had happened to him, including his heart attack, his mind turned to his own family. His heart filled with emotion as he pictured his beautiful daughters, his deceased son and his gentle and supportive partner.

"Wake up David," said Lucy, who was nudging David in the arm.

David had fallen asleep during the last speaker and despite the noise of applause and loud music, David had managed to doze off. Lucy clearly wasn't impressed.

"Come on. It's lunchtime. Let's go and get some air. It looks like you need it."

They headed out through the lobbies still thronging with the crowds huddled around trade stands and purchasing merchandise, courses and books.

The sun was shining, and the brightness of the day contrasted starkly with David's mood. Whilst he had tried to disguise his scepticism from Lucy, falling asleep during one of the talks was clearly not covering up his lack of interest in the proceedings so far.

They walked over to a bench and sat down.

"I knew I should've come with Rosie. She wouldn't be falling asleep. It's embarrassing David. How can you fall asleep when there is so much inspiration all around you?"

"I'm sorry love. It was just the last speaker, I think. Maybe I didn't sleep as well last night as I expected. What was he talking about anyway?"

"The speaker was a she, and she was talking about being the challenges of being a mum and managing a career and trying to be the best at both. Something you'll never understand."

"Oh sorry, yes... what was her name?"

"Bridget Slattery. I'm going to buy her book, even if you do think I'm being gullible."

"I don't think you're gullible at all," David lied. "I'm sure it will be an inspiring read."

"Stop being sarcastic David. If you're going to be a pain in the neck, I'd prefer it if you went back to the hotel and let me attend the rest of the conference!"

"I *am* open-minded honey, but you've got to admit it's a bit of a sales pitch for every speaker isn't it?"

"And what's wrong with that David? They are running a business just like yours and they need to sell their products and services just like you do."

"I guess so," said David sheepishly.

"Look David, everyone here is at different stages of their lives and their personal development journey. Some people may cringe at some speakers whilst others will find them inspirational. It doesn't make any of them better or worse than others. Just different messages for different people, OK?"

David reached out and touched Lucy's hand. "I'm sorry love. I know how important this conference is to you. No, to both of us, so I'll try and stay awake for the next speaker."

"David!" called out a voice from a young man heading towards them. It was John Benjamin and he was waving frantically towards Lucy and David. By the time he'd reached them, David was already on his feet and walking towards John.

"Hey John, it's great to see you. What are you doing here?"

John grabbed David's hand and shook it warmly.

"Good to see you too David. I'm here to hear Craig Thomas speak. He's really good."

Lucy had joined them by this point. "Lucy, this is John Benjamin. I told you about John. He helped me hugely with the business recently and he's now representing one of our biggest suppliers."

"Pleased to meet you John," said Lucy offering her hand towards John, which he took and shook warmly.

"Who is Craig Thomas then John?" said David.

"He has written a book called 'The A+ Factor,'" said John. "It's all about how to remain positive when everything around you is falling apart. It's one of my favourite books, David, and hugely influences how I think and behave. Anyway, how've you been? Is he taking care of himself Lucy?"

"He's a stubborn fool at times John but we're working on him." Lucy was still annoyed with David for falling asleep and his sarcastic remarks about Bridget Slattery.

"Well, I can't stop. Do enjoy your afternoon and remember David, being positive doesn't always *guarantee* a positive outcome, but it does guarantee it will be more positive than if you approach something negatively. See you later!" John skipped away back towards the conference arena.

Lucy broke the awkward silence between them. "He's a nice chap David and I'm glad that you're working with him."

"Yes, he's a decent chap and if he says this guy Craig is worth listening to, then I promise I will this afternoon."

They headed back into the arena and found their seats. The two empty seats previously occupied by Mary and George were now filled with two women who were holding hands. They acknowledged Lucy and David as they squeezed past them and when David sat down in his seat, he turned to the lady next to him.

"Hi, I'm David, have you moved seats?"

"Hi, I'm Victoria and this is my wife, Becky. Nice to meet you David. No, our train from Newcastle was delayed and we ended up missing the morning session. These are our seats though, was someone else sitting here?"

David wondered about Mary and George and why they'd come to the conference.

"Hi Becky," said David shaking her hand. "This is my wife Lucy and the reason we're here."

Lucy shook hands with Becky and Victoria and explained to them what they'd missed in the morning sessions. As David listened, he realised just how much his cynical mind had filtered out and just how impressed he was with Lucy's enthusiasm and ability to recall what had been said.

"Ladies and gentlemen, please take your seats, as the conference will re-commence in 5 minutes."

David suggested he and Lucy swap seats so Lucy could chat more easily with Becky and Victoria, and soon the three of them were chatting away like old friends. David noticed how alive Lucy had become when speaking to the two women and how they shared stories openly about their lives. Lucy managed to tell them all about David, the business, his heart attack and even the journey to get to Birmingham. He was amazed how much information they shared in the short five minutes before the lights started to dim and the music started once more. Dry ice once again emerged from the side of the stage, and Paul and Felicity Stokes appeared again to introduce the next speaker.

After a short introduction, the music went up a notch and Craig Thomas bound onto the stage, pumping his fists in the air. Despite his best efforts, David's enthusiasm for the message he was about to receive was fading quickly. The hype and ceremony which greeted each new speaker just seemed false and unnecessary to him.

"Are you ready to go A+?" boomed Craig from the stage.

There was a roar from the crowd. Everyone except David (or so it felt to him) boomed back at Craig.

"Well, take your seats and let's get positive!"

More cheering, clapping and general whoops and noise came from the crowd and everyone began to sit down, grabbing their notepads, tablets and other devices on which they were going to record the nuggets which 'Being the Best' Craig was going to deliver.

David recalled what John had said and tried to regain some of the positive attitude he knew he needed to get the most from this session.

Craig started talking about himself, his life and how he'd ended up in a very dark place. As he told his story, the crowd began to hush more, and David found himself slowly becoming hooked on Craig's story. It was feeling quite familiar to him and he connected with Craig, as he told the crowd about inheriting his father's business and then encountering, after his father had passed away, a real struggle to keep the business afloat. David knew that feeling well.

Craig then went on to talk about people he'd met who had helped him. Some were strangers and some were people he knew but all of them seemed to say something at the right time or turn up expectedly to give him advice.

David now felt even more that he knew Craig's story.

As the crowd hushed until the auditorium fell completely silent, Craig opened up fully about the darkness that had engulfed him, and he confessed that he had considered taking his own life. As he talked vulnerably about the fear and confusion he'd felt at the time, David was completely transfixed. He could feel his heart beating in his chest as Craig talked about his friend Michael, who had helped him with advice and always seemed to show up when he needed him.

Craig explained how he'd found a reason for living by recognising he was not a bad person to whom bad things happened as some sort of punishment. He turned to his family for inspiration and his daughter had given him a book to read which made him realise he wasn't alone. To gasps from the audience, Craig revealed the book was the Bible. He then went on to explain that he'd found a new faith in something much bigger than him and that this had transformed his life. During the rest of his talk Craig didn't refer to his faith or the Bible. Instead he explained how he'd turned his business around and was hugely helped by the generosity of those around him including his work colleagues, customers and suppliers. Craig's business was in contract catering and he'd managed to secure some large contracts very soon after realising life was not to be feared but to be celebrated and cherished, as though each day was our last. He outlined his steps for an A+ life, including many of the lessons he'd learned from those who'd helped him.

By the time Craig had finished his talk and the crowd had erupted into rapturous applause, David was exhausted. He'd empathised with every step of Craig's story.

"Are you OK love?" shouted Lucy over the cheers still roaring for Craig.

"Of course I am!" said David.

"Why are you crying then?"

David looked at Lucy, smiled and put his arms around her.

"I didn't know I was," he said.

20.

The final two speakers during the afternoon were less interesting to David and even Lucy seemed disappointed in their content, as they both seemed more concerned with selling their books, courses and programmes than they did in delivering some meaningful advice or guidance to the ever-expectant audience.

As David and Lucy began to leave their seats, Becky turned to Lucy and asked her if she wanted to join them for drink in the hotel later. They had already established that they were also staying at the Crowne Plaza. Lucy agreed and turned to David to ask if that was OK.

"Of course it is. I'd love to know your thoughts too on Craig Thomas's talk today. I thought he was incredible!"

"Blimey, you've changed your tune," said Lucy. "From Mr Sceptical to Mr A+ in one afternoon. Miracles do happen then!"

Becky and Victoria laughed out loud and they all headed for the exit.

As David and Lucy walked back in the direction of the hotel, light rain began to fall. Lucy produced a small foldable umbrella from her bag, and they huddled together as they walked.

"Thanks for convincing me to come to this," said David. "I thought Craig's story had so many similarities to my own. It sent shivers up and down my spine. It was spooky wasn't it?"

"You see David; that's the power of empathy. When someone shares their experience openly and without fear of judgement or ridicule, powerful things happen. I loved his story too and could see you were enjoying it. You were transfixed by him!"

"Yes, I was rather hooked. I liked some of his ideas on staying positive, even when everything around you appears to be falling apart. It was also interesting that he referred to the Bible as the book that changed everything for him but then never mentioned it again. I wonder why?"

"I guess nowadays, even if you believe in something, it's not right to ram it down people's throats. Maybe it's more important to hear the words people say than to get hung up on where they've come from or who said them eh?"

"Yes, I think so," said David. "But much of what he spoke about was just common sense which, if he found it in the Bible, why don't more people read it?"

"That's easy to answer," said Lucy. "It's why I won't go to church and why I suspect many people turn away from any form of religion. All religions might be full of great words, but so many people simply don't follow what they signed up to. Maybe that's why these sorts of events are important to us? It might even be speaking some of the same truths you'd find in religious books but in a way that speaks to people rather than preaches at them."

Lucy then laughed and continued: "Maybe we've just been to a new church and didn't even know it!"

David laughed too. "Yes, perhaps the way in which we build our businesses or work together is how we could find a new way to be kind to each other and spread the love."

As they neared the hotel and continued to chat and giggle together, David felt a huge sense of relief and excitement. He'd enjoyed the day and knew the future was bright for him and his family. There was much to be learned from hearing other people's experiences alongside discovering better ways to be in business or build success. He knew he needed to set some new goals for his life based on giving support to others and sharing some of his experiences – just as Craig had done.

"Maybe I could be a speaker at next year's conference!"

"I think you need to become a speaker first David."

"Well, why not? I've a story to tell and maybe it could help others. I might just do that Lucy!"

They skipped into the hotel like excited teenagers and headed up to their room and were soon getting changed and ready for dinner.

They laughed and joked the way through their evening meal and chatted to Becky and Victoria in the bar afterwards. They all agreed that Craig had been the best and most authentic speaker of the day.

By the time David and Lucy headed back to their room, they were high on food and great conversation.

"What a day it's been," said Lucy, as she began to get undressed.

"I know," said David. "I had a slow start, but Craig woke me up and to be honest, if we went home now, I've already gained something magical from the conference. His story was an inspiration. Who's speaking tomorrow Lucy?"

Lucy picked up the programme from the bedside table.

"Apparently, according to the schedule, there is someone called Drew Jones on first. He's a sportsman who won a medal at some Olympics or other. To be honest, I've never heard of him. Then the slot before Robin Anton is the winner of the UK speakers' competition. It will be someone brand new who hasn't spoken at a big event before. Then it's Robin Anton to close the conference."

"Sounds like they've deliberately made the sessions before Robin Anton the weakest to make him look good Lucy!"

"Possibly they have. Do you think it's still worth going to listen to these two speakers or shall we have a lazy breakfast and then take our seats for Robin Anton?"

"I'm fine with that if you are love," said David, walking from the bathroom where he'd been brushing his teeth. As he walked across the bedroom, he noticed something on the floor pushed under the door. He walked over and picked it up. It was a plain red envelope.

"What's that?" asked Lucy.

"I'm not sure honey. It was pushed under our door." David opened the envelope and inside, written on the flap were the words, *Do not judge others and you will not be judged - Matthew 7:1.*

"What's in the envelope David? Is it information about tomorrow?"

David was holding the envelope and staring at the words, which were clearly a quote from the Bible. He knew it was an important message but didn't want to alarm Lucy by trying to explain the significance to her of another red envelope. He wondered if the message was encouraging him not to dismiss the first two speakers of the morning.

"It's just a reminder to everyone to make sure they are in their seats on time for the start of the day tomorrow. I think we do need to go along to the first two speakers love. Drew might have something important to say, and the winner of the speakers' competition deserves a full hall to speak to don't you think?"

"Yes, I guess so. OK, we'll go along to the first two sessions. Now come and join me in this big bed, I'm feeling lonely in here!"

David folded up envelope and placed it in the drawer next to his bed. He turned over and cuddled up to Lucy, with excitement about what the next day would bring.

"I love you Lucy Turner. Thanks for bringing me along to your fabulous conference."

"My pleasure," said Lucy.

They drifted gently into a warm and contented sleep.

21.

When David woke up the next morning, Lucy was still sleeping soundly. David got up to head towards the shower and decided he should remove the red envelope from his drawer so Lucy wouldn't find it and be worried by its unusual lack of contents and biblical reference. He gently pulled open the drawer, not wishing to disturb Lucy, and unfolded the red envelope. He opened the flap to read the phrase again which said, *Faith shows the reality of what we hope for; it is the evidence of things we cannot see. Hebrews 11.1*

David sat staring at the envelope. He knew the passage in the envelope was not the same as the one he'd read the previous evening. Last night the message told him not to judge others and this morning, it was to have faith in things he couldn't see. David's heart was pounding in his chest and he could feel cold sweat on his brow. He gripped the side of the bed and took a deep breath, slowing his breathing and calming himself.

"Morning gorgeous."

David quickly folded the envelope into his hand so Lucy couldn't see it. "Morning lovely lady, how are you this fine morning? Did you sleep well?"

"Like a log – best sleep I've had in ages. Did you?"

"Yes, great," David lied. He'd been tossing and turning all night with strange dreams about deep conversations with Michael, but he couldn't recall anything Michael had said. He'd woken up just as Michael was about to introduce him to his boss.

"I'm going to jump in the shower love. You take your time to wake up as we've got a big day ahead."

David showered, shaved and dressed while Lucy was still lying in her bed checking her mobile phone.

"I've checked in with the girls. All is well at home," said Lucy.

"We've only been gone 24 hours, they'll be fine." David loved how much Lucy constantly thought about the girls. She'd always been protective, but after Peter died, she'd become even more protective and really didn't like to leave the girls, especially when they had been younger.

"I'm going for a quick walk while you're getting ready. I need to keep up my exercise, don't I?"

"Sure, OK. I won't be long getting ready so don't be too long on your walk. We can go and grab some breakfast when you're back."

David kissed her on the cheek, left the room, walked along the corridor and headed for the hotel reception and exit. He knew the hotel was near the convention centre and there were paths and a lake he could walk around. Just as he was passing through the exit doors, he heard a voice call his name from behind him.

"David Turner, as I live and breathe!"

David turned around quickly to see someone waving madly to him across the reception area. He recognised him immediately as Andy Smith, who had bullied David incessantly for four years at the secondary school they'd both attended. David's heart skipped a beat and he immediately awaited some snide or sarcastic remark from this nemesis from years ago.

"David! How are you me old mate? Gosh it must be twenty years since we were at school together."

David noticed that Andy was limping as he walked towards him but was more concerned about the memories stirring uncomfortably around this man who'd made his teenage years a total misery.

"Hold up a second will you, this old man can't run so quick nowadays."

Andy eventually caught up with David and they stood together just outside the doors of the hotel. Andy put out his hand to shake David's and there was an uncomfortable pause while David's brain kicked in and his manners overtook his sense of foreboding at the encounter with this distasteful memory from the past.

"Hi Andy. Good to see you. How are you?"

David was hoping to offer the minimum of pleasantries so he could leave the slimy memory behind and get on with his walk.

"I'm great thanks. Are you going for a morning stroll? Can I join you?"

"I guess so."

The two men began to walk away from the hotel towards the lake in the grounds of the convention centre.

"So, David, what have you been doing with yourself over all these years? Last time we were at school together you reckoned your future was all sorted, as you were going to join your dad's plumbing business. Did you step into your dad's shoes?"

David was already irritated. Andy would constantly tell all his friends that David was born with a silver spoon in his mouth and therefore his future was all sorted with no effort on his part. He even created a nickname for David, referring to him as 'The Tube,' referring to the plumbing business he was destined to inherit.

'Nobody could step into my dad's shoes Andy and I certainly didn't."

"How is the old boy then? Still running his tube and tap business, is he?"

"No, my dad died some years ago thanks Andy."

"Oh sorry, I didn't know mate. We've not shared the same circles for some time, so I missed that."

"Yes, you did. But I guess you weren't to know. It's OK."

They strolled together in a few moments of silence under the growing warmth of the morning sunshine. In the momentary silence, David recalled the first passage written on the inside of the red envelope he'd received the previous evening. He realised perhaps he was judging this old school friend too harshly.

"Yes, Dad did die and yes, I did take over the business, but it's been no easy ride I can tell you!"

"Yeah, I know I used to give you a hard time when we were at school didn't I? I was right out of order to be honest mate. I never meant any harm by it you know."

David didn't believe him. He recalled vividly how Andy and his mates would push and poke him in the dinner queue, calling him The Tube and deliberately trip him up in the corridors. He remembered going home after school and dreading the next day, as he knew it would follow the same format as the last.

"It was pretty tough to be honest Andy. I didn't enjoy school much and you and your mates were pretty much the main reason." David was trying to be civil but was struggling to keep deep-rooted feelings from beginning to surface after such a long time.

"Ouch. I hear you David. You're probably wondering why I was such an arsehole back then. Will you let me apologise?"

David's walking pace had quickened, and it was clear Andy was struggling to keep up. Part of David wanted to walk faster and as far away from this bully from his past as he could.

Andy put his hand on David's arm. "Can we stop a second David? My leg is giving me some real gip this morning." He signalled to a bench at the side of the path.

"Can we sit down for a second David, so I can explain."

David's heartbeat was fast and, in some ways, furious. Why had this memory from his childhood surfaced just at a time he was starting to feel more positive about the future? He really wasn't ready to be having deep conversations with an old school bully.

"I don't mean to be rude Andy, but school was a long time ago and I'd really prefer to just complete my walk before the conference starts."

"Oh wow, you're at the conference too then? That's amazing. Come on David, let's sit down. I think I've got some explaining to do and all I want you to do is listen with an open mind OK?"

Reluctantly, and still determined to finish his walk alone, David sat down next to Andy on the bench. As he did so, he caught sight of why Andy was limping. Poking out of the top of his training shoe was a metal leg. Andy had clearly lost his foot and part of his leg at some point. David suddenly felt guilty about Andy. Something awful had happened to Andy and yet he had spent the past few minutes judging him for something from a long time ago.

"Andy, do go on. I'm listening."

"Thanks for listening David. Back then, I was a prize idiot at school. I was jealous of lots of kids and especially you. I'd always wanted my dad to be a successful person like your dad but instead he spent most of his time down the pub getting pissed. When he was at home, he'd spend the rest of the time knocking ten bells out of my mum. There was many a time when I had to clean up the mess he'd leave behind after an all-night bender and then I'd have to come to school."

"Gosh, I never knew, Andy."

"No one knew, David, not even the teachers. I just got on with it, along with my two younger brothers and baby sister. There were many mornings when I had to feed them and get them dressed while Mum dealt with the bruises and Dad dealt with another hangover. I'd come to school and look for someone to blame or someone who I could take out my anger on and I'm afraid you were it: the perfect kid with the perfect family. I didn't see why you had it easy while I had it hard. I picked on you to make myself feel better. It's time for me to apologise to you David. I'm so sorry I was such an idiot and hope it didn't affect you too badly."

"It's cool," lied David. "The past is the past and I guess we must move on with our lives as you have done, and I have done too."

Andy stood up and was about to leave but David wanted to find out more about this man who he'd harshly judged. "I've got to head back to the conference now David, but I'm glad I bumped into you. It's good to find some forgiveness for the shit things we've done in our lives. I might see you after the conference, but I've got a pretty big day ahead, so I hope you enjoy it. It was a genuine blessing to have met you this morning and to be able to say sorry. Thanks for accepting my apology."

Andy put out his hand to shake David's. David grabbed his hand, standing up as he did so. "Thanks for your apology Andy and yes, it's fully accepted. I wish now that I'd known what you were going through. I may have been able to help."

"Sometimes we have to experience things alone David. Our lessons in life are always our own, even if we do travel through life with others. Take care of yourself and I have a feeling we'll see each other again soon enough."

Andy was already limping away from David towards the conference centre before he had chance to ask when they could meet up for a coffee. He sat back down on the bench, his mind was racing with memories of Andy and the times he'd come to school looking scruffy and with the wrong kit for the day's sports activity. He remembered how he had looked down on Andy as a waste of a life and someone who would amount to nothing. It was clear now just how little he knew about the real Andy Smith. As he sat on a bench in the park thinking about Andy, Michael came back into his mind and in the silence of his mind he heard Michael say the words, "Do not judge others and you will not be judged." David recognised the words, as they had been on the inside of the red envelope the previous evening.

David lowered his head and felt a sense of shame. He'd judged Andy right up to the point he'd listened to him to hear his story. David sensed there was far more to his story than he had told him during their brief encounter. He vowed to find Andy after the conference and spend more time getting to know the poor lost boy who had once bullied him at school.

David slowly rose from the bench and headed back to the hotel to meet Lucy, who was waiting for him in the reception area looking very worried.

"Where've you been? You didn't take your mobile phone with you so I couldn't get hold of you. I was worried. We've not got time for breakfast now as we need to head over to the conference."

"Sorry honey, I bumped into an old school friend and we started chatting about his past and mine. It was quite an eye opener Lucy. It made me realise just how easily we judge the lives of others without having ever really knowing what is going on behind their troubled eyes."

"Well, this all sounds very deep and meaningful David, but we need to get across to the convention centre now. You'll need to grab a coffee from a booth on the way in. Come on."

Lucy took David by the arm and started to walk them both purposefully towards the convention centre. During the short distance Andy wasn't mentioned again and instead, Lucy told David how she'd met up with Becky and Victoria over breakfast and how they all chatted about the conference and who was their favourite speaker. Becky told Lucy that Drew Jones was a great speaker and that she'd heard him tell his story before. She said Lucy and David were in for a treat.

This lifted the spirits of them both as they entered the arena, grabbing a coffee for David on the way and finding their seats where Becky and Victoria were already waiting for them.

The dry ice was soon appearing on stage and the music rose to a loud crescendo of cheers and clapping as Felicity and Paul Stokes once again took to the stage. They outlined the programme for the day, which would begin with Drew Jones the Olympic athlete, and then be followed by the mystery speaker and winner of the UK speaking competition. Then Robin Anton would close the Be the Best conference.

They asked for hush from the expectant crowd and Paul Stokes began to introduce Drew Jones.

"Drew grew up in difficult circumstances where his family life was dysfunctional and disrupted by alcohol and violence. He watched his father go to prison for causing grievous bodily harm to his mother and then decided he needed to do something more positive with his life... but we'll let Drew tell you the rest... Ladies and gentlemen, please welcome to the stage – Drew Jones!"

The crowd erupted and everyone stood to their feet as Drew Jones walked slowly across the stage. David grabbed Lucy by the arm. "Oh my God, it's Andy…"

"Yes, I know who it is. They've just introduced him David, it's Drew Jones."

David was shaking his head. "No… No… his name is Andy Smith – I went to school with him."

The audience began to calm down and Drew waved to get everyone to sit down, as he went behind a lectern to speak. David was still holding Lucy's arm, but he was shaking.

"Oh my God…" he whispered.

Drew Jones looked up from the lectern. "Ladies and gentlemen. Sometimes in life we get chances to make amends and sometimes those opportunities are taken away from us. Not by actions but by judgement. Often, we seek forgiveness from those we've hurt and sometimes forgiveness isn't given to us. But I'm here to tell you, every one of you in the arena this morning is capable of seizing two vitally important opportunities. The first is to recognise that you always get the chance to try again; to put right what is wrong in your life and to try again, even when you think you've failed. Every one of us has a God-given right be to be offered another chance. The second opportunity for everyone in this room is to forgive those who've wronged you. Not just to accept an apology but to fully, completely and totally forgive those who've hurt you. I'm living proof this is possible, and I've taken both opportunities and grasped them with both hands. I hope my talk this morning will help you to do the same."

The arena had fallen into a reflective hush and other than the odd cough or noise from outside the arena, a quietness had quickly descended, and people started to whisper. Lucy whispered to David.

"This is going to be amazing David and I think you're going to love his story."

David didn't say anything at all. He was simply staring at his school friend Andy Smith who was on the stage at the Be the Best conference and had been talking to him just a few minutes earlier. But his name was not Drew Jones. David was confused but transfixed by the man on stage.

"You see," said Andy, "I had a tough start in life. My father is an alcoholic and he would often come home after a couple of days hitting the booze and take out his anger on my mum. Many times, I had to pull him off my mum, as there was a real chance that he'd kill her. I'd then help my younger brothers and sister get dressed and ready for school. I was just sixteen years of age. I'd go to school and take out my frustration on others. No one knew why I was angry, and I became a bully to anyone I thought had a better life than me. But, ladies and gentlemen, just this morning I bumped into one of the people I bullied at school. He's here at this conference sitting somewhere amongst you. I had no idea he'd be here, and I know he had no idea I'd be speaking to you today. But we talked, and he listened, and he offered me forgiveness. He released me from my shame this morning and I hope that my apology healed him too."

David was shaking in his seat. Lucy looked worried. "Are you OK love, you look pale. Are you sure you're alright?"

"He's talking about me Lucy. We met this morning... I'm the one he bullied at school... he's talking about me Lucy."

"Gosh, are you serious? Drew was who you were chatting to on your walk?"

"Yes. It was Andy, his name is Andy Smith, not Drew Jones."

"You might be feeling sorry for the sixteen-year-old boy," Andy continued. "Or you may be thinking your life has been worse. Or you may right now be remembering someone who bullied you and wondering why they did so. You see, ladies and gentlemen, we all have a story. We all have a past. We all have periods in our lives that can break us. But they can make us too. As mine did for me."

A ripple of polite applause broke out in the crowd. People around David were grabbing notebooks or opening their iPads and phones to make notes, everyone certain Drew Jones was going to continue to deliver some powerful messages to be remembered for future use.

Lucy had taken her notebook out of her bag and Becky and Victoria did the same. David just sat in silence and anticipation.

Andy went on to tell his story of how his father had eventually been arrested for harming his mother and went to prison for five years. During that time Andy had joined the Royal Engineers in the British Army. He'd done so partly to get away from his previous life, but also because he'd not been able to hold down a full-time job for much longer than a few months. His short temper would usually end up in a fight with another employee and his subsequent instant dismissal. Someone had suggested the army would be good for him, so he took them at their word and signed up, completing the necessary medical tests with ease.

With the audience in total silence and transfixed by his story, he went on to explain he'd been stationed in Iraq during 2011, just as the war was coming to an end. But during a brief bomb search, a landmine had exploded and killed two of his fellow soldiers. In the blast, Andy had lost his leg below the knee.

He then recalled how in hospital back in the UK recovering, a man named Michael had visited him, saying he was the hospital chaplain. Michael had told him a story about a farmer and a horse.

David took Lucy's hand and squeezed it tightly.

The crowd listened intently as Andy recounted the story and how he realised he had to look at what had happened to him as neither good nor bad. When he had recovered and just after his prosthetic leg had been fitted, one of the officers who came to visit him during his recovery told him about the Paralympic Games. Andy knew he had to make something of his life, so he began training and getting fit.

"You see, ladies and gentlemen, things happen in life over which we've no control. But the one aspect of our lives over which we do have control is how we respond to those situations which, on the surface may appear to be setbacks or even disasters, but which can turn out to be the biggest opportunity of our lives."

Suddenly, a video screen lit up behind Andy. It was a video of him competing in the 400m relay at the Paralympic Games and he was on the final lap. As the video progressed, the commentator was clearly favouring the US team who were, by the time it got to Andy's turn to run, over 10 metres ahead of him. The crowd watched as Andy took the baton from his teammates and started to run, swinging his metal leg around with each stride. As the commentator's voice rose with excitement, so did the crowd in the arena, and people began cheering Andy on, even though it was a video recording of a past event.

Andy continued to gain ground on the leading athlete, overtaking various other athletes until he was right on the shoulder of the leading runner. The crowd in the video and the crowd in the arena were screaming encouragement and as Andy just got to the point where he was about to gain the lead, the runner ahead of him found a burst of energy and finished first, with Andy coming in second just a few steps behind.

There were gasps and groans from both crowds, as they watched Andy run straight to the winner and throw his arms around him in a gesture of comradeship and congratulations. The video moved on to the medal ceremony where the flags of the USA, Great Britain and Spain were raised against the backdrop of the American national anthem. When the silver medal was presented to Andy, the camera focused on Andy and it was clear that tears were rolling down his cheeks.

As the crowd in the arena began to settle, Andy returned to the lectern.

"So, who won the race? Yes, it was James Adderley from the USA who came first, and I came second. But who really won? The answer is simple, ladies and gentlemen. It was the human spirit. For everyone competing, the mere act of running a race, throwing a javelin or jumping into a sandpit, was enough. You see, we were all simply aiming to finish our events, but still settling for nothing less than our best. For many of us, our best was simply to get out of bed every day and train, until our limbs, our minds and our spirits were empty and exhausted. Michael once said to me while I was lying in hospital that too many people seek more and bigger things in their lives to make them happy. But being the best, which is the title of this conference, isn't always about coming first. It's not always about getting the gold medal or the highest marks. It's not always about having the biggest house, fastest car or most prestigious job. Sometimes, when we aim to be the best parent we can be, the best husband, wife, son, daughter, brother or sister we can be, this will bring far greater happiness than larger or more plentiful possessions. You see, ladies and gentlemen, there was a prize far greater than the medal I was awarded. It was the fact that my father was there to see it. Ladies and gentlemen, please welcome to the stage, my dad, Trevor Smith."

The audience gasped and there were cheers and shouting as Andy embraced his father on stage. David looked at Lucy and she was crying, as were Becky and Victoria, who were embracing each other. David stood in awe and wonder at what he'd just heard.

As the crowd settled once more, it was Trevor who took the microphone.

"Ladies and gentlemen, thank you for allowing me to take a few moments of Andy's talk. But it's important you know why I'm here. When I was let out of prison, Andy was in Iraq on military service. The first time I saw him was in hospital after he'd lost his leg. I went to the hospital to ask for his forgiveness. Yes, I'm an alcoholic and I will be for the rest of my days, but in prison I'd been four years without a drink, and I'd committed to myself to make up for the awful mess I'd made of my family. My wife, Andy's mother, had divorced me while I was in prison and had found a lovely new man in her life who was taking much better care of her than I had ever done. But before I asked for her forgiveness, I needed to ask forgiveness from the son who time and time again had washed me down when I was covered in vomit, had intervened when I was hurting his mother, and had been the dad to his brothers and sisters I'd never been. I needed his forgiveness."

David looked at Lucy and she was weeping gently and held his hand more tightly. He was struggling to hold back a wave of emotion in danger of bursting through his chest.

"When I arrived at the hospital and asked to see my son, I discovered he'd changed his name from Andy Smith to Drew Jones, as he'd wanted nothing to connect him to me. As I walked towards my broken son, I knew I was a broken man who deserved nothing but Andy's anger and dismissal. But as I walked towards him, he simply said these words: 'Hello Dad, I forgive you…'"

As Trevor said the final few words, his voice broke with emotion and Andy embraced his father once more. The crowd erupted into cheers, shouts and more tears. Lucy grabbed David's arm and held his hand more tightly. Becky and Victoria were holding each other tightly and silently weeping together.

David was still struggling to hold onto the emotion rising within his chest.

Andy moved from behind the lectern and was now standing at the front of the stage.

"But, ladies and gentlemen, let me tell you why my first words to my father were to forgive him. You see, it's often far harder to hold onto something than it is to let it go. I knew neither of us could change the past. I couldn't bring back my leg and Dad couldn't erase the harm he'd done to my mum or his kids. But we *could* start again. And to do so, I had to take the second opportunity, which was to forgive someone. I went on to forgive those who planted the mines that killed my friends and took away my leg. I forgave those teachers who told me I'd never do anything with my life. I realised, holding on to anger and resentment is like drinking poison and expecting someone else to die. Often those we're angry with have moved on with their lives and yet we remain stuck in our anger and resentment, drinking the poison every day. So, I made a deal with my father. If he could stay off the booze, I wanted him to help me to compete at the Paralympic Games. You see, it was never about winning a medal for me; it was about simply having another chance to succeed at something and to do it with those I loved. When I crossed the finish line in second place, I knew I'd won the most important race of my life. It was the race to take on board what life had thrown at me and make the best of it. And it was to take the opportunity to rebuild a relationship many in this arena will never get the chance to do. Don't waste your lives in regret or anger. Live your life open to opportunity and ready to forgive. Because if you do, you'll win your race by being the best you can be. Thank you."

The arena erupted. People rushed towards the stage and were applauding above their heads. Andy and Trevor held hands aloft as the audience continued to cheer. Many were hugging their friends or family and Lucy hugged David, who was now crying uncontrollably. The emotion of Andy's story and the realisation he'd judged him so harshly, not knowing the full story about to unfold, was too much for David to hold in. He thought about his own father and just how much he wanted to tell him how much he loved him, and he wept. And the entire arena wept with him.

22.

As they descended the stairs from the arena to grab some refreshments, everyone was talking about Andy Smith. Many were still wiping the tears from their eyes with a sense of wonder at what had just happened.

"Gosh, that was quite an experience Lucy and so inspiring wasn't it?"

"Yes, I could hardly stand up by the time Andy had finished. My legs have gone to jelly!"

"I'm sorry I doubted you and this event. It's been incredible. I can see why people come to hear the stories of people who've had such eventful lives. It makes our lives seem very ordinary by comparison."

"But maybe we shouldn't compare. You run a business, have built a family, lost a son, had a heart attack and are looking to move forward again. Some would say, comparing our lives with others is futile anyway. Every life is unique isn't it?"

David remembered something Tony had said whilst they were chatting in their hospital beds. He'd said many people had a crippling disease called 'comparisonitis,' which had made David laugh at the time. Tony said many people wanted more just so that they could be like their friends or neighbours. It was driving people into debt, constantly wanting more rather than being happy with what they had.

Tony was a perfect example of someone aiming for less but gaining far more.

"Yes Lucy, we often compare our lives with others and think ours are easier, harder, more exciting or more boring when really they are all simply unique."

The coffee booths, bookstores and shops were all bustling and there was an air of excitement hanging in the air. Andy Smith had made a huge impact on those who'd heard him talk, just as he had those who saw him at the Paralympics. David admired his old friend and wished he'd had the chance to find out more about his story on his walk. David rebuked himself for the wasted time he'd spent in judgement of his old friend, and the words in the red envelope returned to haunt David as they made their way back into the arena for the mystery speaker.

Once they'd taken their seats again, David found himself recalling all the events of the past few weeks in his life. He thought about Michael and still wasn't sure who he was, but it seemed that many people had also met the same man. He seemed to turn up at just the right moment with the right advice for the right situation. While part of David wanted to imagine Michael as some sort of angel or guide, his years of cynicism prevented him from accepting this. Without proof, things do not exist, he thought to himself.

Lucy interrupted his thoughts.

"I wonder who this mystery speaker will be David? They must be good if they've won a speaking competition."

David was still thinking about Michael, but the now familiar sound of music and spectacle dry ice began as Felicity and Paul Stokes returned to the stage once more.

"Did you enjoy Drew Jones?" bellowed Paul from the stage. "What a great example of how to Be the Best, just what this conference is all about. Now we've something a little different. Our next speaker will be someone you've not heard from before. This is his debut on a professional stage after winning the UK Speakers Association award for best newcomer at our awards last month. This award is given to the person who shows the greatest promise as a new speaker. The title of his talk is *The 10 Steps to Real Success,* so please give a warm Be the Best welcome to John Benjamin!

The crowd offered warm if reserved applause as a young man nervously walked across the stage. David recognised him immediately.

"That's John Benjamin!" he shouted.

People around David and Lucy turned and wondered why he had stated the obvious. David turned to Lucy. "But it's John Benjamin," he said again.

"Yes love, Paul Stokes has just announced him. Are you OK?"

"Yes of course I'm OK but that's John Benjamin! You know, you met him yesterday. He's the main reason why our business turned around. Don't you remember? We saw him yesterday! Am I going to end up knowing everyone on this stage today?"

Everyone around David and Lucy were taking their seats and wondering why David was so animated. They sat down and Lucy held David's arm.

"Yes, I do remember him," she whispered. "He seemed a really nice young man so let's see what he has to say then shall we?"

The lights dimmed until there was one single spotlight on John. He was wearing a dark pinstripe suit, a waistcoat, a white shirt with an old-fashioned pin-collar with two studs on both sides and a dark blue tie matching his suit. In his breast pocket, a crisp white handkerchief poked out. He was wearing black brogue shoes and David felt a tinge of pride to see his young friend on the stage.

But John didn't say anything. A few seconds turned into thirty seconds and then a minute and John was just standing on the stage. Whispers began to build around the arena and people shifted uncomfortably in their seats. Victoria leaned towards Lucy.

"Do you think he's got stage fright?"

Another ten seconds elapsed and then John spoke.

"Silence."

The whispering died down again and another few seconds pause. There was a sense of anticipation amongst the audience.

"Silence," said John again. "Silence is the space in between your thoughts and it's where your greatest thoughts exist. But too often, in your busy world, you're too noisy to hear the silence."

The crowd hushed and the hall was quiet. David could hear his own breathing as he waited for what John was going to say next.

"Ladies and gentlemen, if you will give me twenty minutes of your silence, I will share with you ten steps for living which will transform your lives and bring you real success in a way you never thought possible. I will speak without a break and I respectfully ask you to listen carefully to what I say. For what I say comes from the highest authority. So, let me begin."

People were looking at each other, wondering what this enigmatic young speaker was going to say. His brave use of silence at the beginning of his talk had made a powerful point. Notepads, phones and iPads were all coming out for the audience to take notes.

John looked up from the lectern.

"Step one is to find the silence. Seek a place where your thoughts are unhindered and uninhibited by the noise of your daily routine. Spend time in nature or simply spend time alone and allow your mind to quieten down from the constant internal chatter. The silence is the gateway to your deepest thoughts, and it will direct and guide you. Beyond the silence is your intuition, which is the place of true knowing. Your ego will drown out this most gentle voice, so recognise its sound and feel its presence. Your silence and intuition live in your heart and not your head. To find the most knowing part of who you are, you must first find the silence between your thoughts."

The hall had indeed fallen silent and David was blown away by John's assured speaking. All around him, people were making notes and listening intently to what the young man was saying. John hadn't moved a muscle since he first stood behind the lectern. His steady and calm manner, together with the eerie silence in the room, created a heady cocktail of anticipation and respect.

"Step two," said John. "Trust in synchronicity. As you begin to consider your future and reconnect with who you really are, people will come into your life at the right time and often with a message you need to hear. Listen for the conversations and watch for the connections. There are no such things as chance or coincidence. You're part of something so much bigger than yourself. There will be moments when you may dismiss a chance meeting as irrelevant, or a short conversation as unimportant. But if you listen to your intuition and the silence of your thoughts, you will hear the significance. Be open to the impossible and watch the possible emerge in your life."

David looked around the arena. Everywhere he looked, people were scribbling in their notebooks or tapping away on their devices.

"Step three is to seek your purpose first. Too many of you search for your joy, your happiness and your success in boxes, bags and stuff. You set huge goals and ambitions about amassing more, bigger and better possessions and greater comfort in your life. But life is meant to be uncomfortable. The Comfort Zone is the most dangerous place to live and yet many of you spend your lives there. Remember, when you're thinking about your future, you should always start with what you love in the present, and this can be found within your true purpose. Your life purpose is why you're here today. It's what drives you to be the best you can be. Your purpose has four pillars, each of which has a part to play in your future success and happiness. The first pillar is called passion. You must consider what you're truly passionate about. What causes, activities or places can you be, where you forget time? When are you reading or studying and simply never get bored? What positive difference do you want to make to the world? Your purpose is not going to be found within something that doesn't interest you. Your life has not been created that way. You were created to find your passion."

David was nodding and listening and wondering. This young man who he'd thought he knew, was holding the attention of over a thousand people, who were listening to his every word. No one in the audience was speaking.

Lucy was busy scribbling notes, as were Becky and Victoria. In fact, all around David, people were making notes. David was just listening.

"The next pillar of your purpose is your talents. What are you good at? What can you do easily that others find more difficult? This doesn't need to be a specific technical skill. Often people say they don't possess any talents and yet they care for others with genuine ease, or they listen so well that others talk to them or go to them for guidance. If you're unsure of your talents, ask others what they see within you that perhaps you can't see for yourself. Your purpose is not to spend your life struggling to accomplish something for which you clearly have no natural ability. Sure, it's good to test yourselves and learn new skills, but your purpose should be to use the talents you have first."

Lucy leant over and whispered to David. "I've no idea what I'm good at, so you're going to need to help me out with that one!"

David smiled, as he instantly thought about how her caring nature, willingness to listen, and her ability to stick at something when he would quit too quickly. John was right. We often can't see our natural talents, as they are exactly that – natural to us.

"You see, your talents are often hidden in your blind spots," said John. "The very nature of your natural talents is that you're not aware you possess them. This is why we need others to point them out."

"He's right," whispered Lucy again. "I've no idea where my blind spots are!"

David smiled.

John moved out from behind the lectern for the first time and walked towards the edge of the stage. "And remember, other people have talents too, so focus on what you're good at and allow others to use their unique talents to help you."

The cameras being used to project the image of the speakers onto two large screens at the back of stage had closed in on John's face. His eyes were pale blue, and they stared out across the audience. David was convinced John wasn't blinking, such was the authority with which he looked out across the arena.

John lowered his voice. "Your third pillar of purpose is to understand and articulate your core values. Your values are what drive you and within them you uncover what is important to you. They're your moral compass and will direct your decision making, your responses and your choices. When you're misaligned with your values, your own moral compass will be working against you. Therefore, many people struggle at work or in their businesses. When you're asked to work or behave in a way out of line with your values, you'll never be able to fully succeed in a way that will bring you true fulfilment. Live in line with your values, as your purpose is not held within actions contrary to them."

The arena was now almost completely silent. David noticed the whirring of the air conditioning for the first time. The young man on stage was captivating the entire audience and a sense of calm authority was evident again. He lowered his voice still further and stepped right to the edge of the stage.

"But most of all, you must find your connection. Your highest calling is already within you. It may not be a vocation or a place to visit in the world. It will be something that comes back into your mind, time and time again. It will often be a random thought appearing in the silence of your deepest thoughts. Your calling will whisper to you; it will never shout your name. It's there in the simplest of ways, so don't try to overcomplicate your calling, for we all have one. Some may experience many callings through their lives but each time they will feel connected to something much bigger than themselves when they are responding to it. It is through your calling you connect to your highest self, your divine self. But you don't need to seek it. Allow it to find you and in time, it will."

John walked back to the lectern. "I've given you the first three steps for real success. Let me now add a fourth. It is this: aim for less. Find joy in the small things. This is not to say you shouldn't have ambitions or settle for less than you can achieve, and yes, you can have big dreams. But work out the small steps along the way and celebrate these. Recognise that always wanting more means you always put off the feeling of achievement to a later day. Just look around you at the wonder of your world. Notice the small things people do that make you happy. Recognise it's the smallest of acts that can make the largest of impacts. To illustrate this, let me tell you the story of the Mexican fisherman."

David's attention rose even further.

John continued.

"One day, a Harvard business graduate was on holiday in Mexico. He was walking along a wooden pier when he came across a fisherman who, using a single line, was catching fish. In a basket next to him were a few beautiful fresh fish he'd caught. The Harvard graduate asked the fisherman how long he'd been fishing for. 'Maybe a few hours', he replied. 'Gosh, you're good', said the Harvard graduate. 'Why don't you aim for more, put a second line down and double the amount of fish you catch?' The fisherman turned to the Harvard graduate and asked, 'OK, you clearly are a clever man, so why would I do that?' The Harvard graduate was keen to share his business knowledge with this simple fisherman, so he responded. 'Well my friend, once you've doubled your output, you could purchase a small boat and go out to sea where there are more fish, lay down nets and catch even more fish.' The fisherman looked round once more. 'OK clever man, what happens then?' Our Harvard man was in his stride now. 'Well, then you can raise your game by purchasing more boats and employing some staff. You could even create a fishing company!' 'OK senor', said the Mexican. 'And what happens then?' Harvard man was now bouncing with enthusiasm. 'Then it gets really exciting my friend. You expand your fishing company into a fleet of boats, fishing all over the world every day of the year, amassing a great fortune.' The fisherman turned around once more. 'OK senor, if I do all these things you say, what happens then?' The man from Harvard looked pleased with himself and his willing student. 'Well then my friend, you get to retire to a little Mexican fishing village and sit on the pier all day catching fish.'"

For the first time, the audience burst into polite applause. There was no cheering or shouting but it was clear the audience had picked up the message from the story.

"You see, my friends, aiming for less doesn't mean a life of low achievement. But it does mean choosing congruent goals that bring you the *feeling* of happiness, because happiness is a feeling and not a thing that comes with acquiring more and more in your life."

The audience applauded again. John had them in the palm of his hand and David looked on with a mixture of pride and awe. He was impressed with the young man's ability to capture the attention of the room. It reminded David of the story of Jesus when he was a young man in the temple. While David couldn't recall all the story that he'd heard in his childhood, there was something going on in the room which was equally impressive.

John moved from behind the lectern again.

"Step five, ladies and gentlemen, is a simple one. Realise that sometimes it's your move. You live on a planet within a universe you barely understand, and so often you fail to recognise you're not living in isolation. Everything is connected and sometimes the universe you inhabit steps back to allow you to decide where to move in your life. The best place to gain guidance when you're wondering where your life is heading, is within the silence. It's here that you can access your own intuition. This will often whisper to you that it's time to move in a different direction. Our lives are like a huge game of chess where at times, we appear to be in a place where we can't escape. But while we've breath in our lungs, there is always a move we can make. It may not be easy, and it may not always be pleasant, but my friends, the immense power at work around you may place you in a position where you simply must make a move. Just like the situation called 'check' in chess, where there is always at least a single move we can make, sometimes we must simply accept the nudge and move on."

David remembered what Mel had said about the game of chess in the park she'd seen with Michael and Mary. He wondered if John had seen them too.

"Step six," John continued, "is to look out for the weeds that choke your dreams. Often, when we've listened to the silence, heard our intuition, built our pillars of purpose and made our moves, we can encounter blockages in our path. These could be real encounters that seem to get in our way or simply the negative thoughts that seek to trip us up. When you sow your dreams into fertile soil, the weeds of doubt and fear can grow too. The closer you get to building your life around your purpose or the nearer you are to making an important step, the more you may encounter forces that seek to stop you. Celebrate this my friends, for it is the greatest sign that you're close to something important. Keep your eyes on your dreams, trust your senses, listen to the silence and press on. The forces of good that support your life will always be with you, so allow your connection to your divine self to propel you to victory over fear."

David remembered their journey to Birmingham. He could now see just how important it had been for him to get to the 'Be the Best' conference. He could see how his belief that all would be well was not some blind faith or pig-headed unwillingness to accept the doubts or blockages in his path. Instead, it was his inner knowing that all would be well. David shivered as if someone had stepped over him.

"Well done son."

David twisted round to see who had spoken to him, but everyone around him was making notes and was transfixed by the young man on the stage.

"There are four more steps to follow for a happy life full of real success. Step seven is not to judge others until you know their story. A wise man who lived over two thousand years ago once said, 'He who has no sin cast the first stone'. You've forgotten this simple truth that we're all broken. None of us is without fault, shame or error. And yet often you seek to judge someone for their past, their current choices or simply because they are different to you. It is often easier to judge and more difficult to recognise your own transgressions. But you must acknowledge these first to know what is behind the eyes of those you seek to condemn. Your story has shaped you. Respect that others' stories have shaped them and then love them rather than condemn them."

The arena was silent. The young man was captivating. He spoke with such calm authority that people would doubt his years. But his messages were familiar; not just to David but to many in the arena. Some had heard them from others, handed down from generations, some had heard them from Michael and his friends, just as David had.

"Step eight is to know that forgiveness can be the gateway to your greatest progress. Many of you hold onto pain, to anger and to grudges against those who've been cruel, unfair or violent towards you. Whilst you don't need to accept their behaviour or condone it, you can forgive them. You may have to move away from them or from a situation to fully heal yourself. If you hold onto the pain they've caused you, then you are the one who carries the poison in your heart. It is *your* body and your mind that becomes clogged with the memories, the frustration and the uncomfortable feelings that linger long after the acts you need to forgive. And remember – the most important person to forgive is yourself. You will have made mistakes, said the wrong things, made the wrong decisions and looked back in hindsight with regret. But hindsight takes you nowhere unless you convert it into renewed action. At that point it becomes wisdom."

David turned to Lucy and whispered, "Maybe it's time to forgive myself for the way the business had become and for the state of our finances."

Lucy squeezed his arm. "You're the only person who still looks back on those decisions, David. The rest of us moved on a long time ago."

John had started to move across the stage. His hair shone under the lights and as he stood to the right-hand side of the stage, a spotlight surrounded him with a pool of light. David smiled and wondered if a light was shining directly from heaven, as he watched on in awe at the young man sharing his wisdom.

"Step nine is simple. Love is all there is. When all is said and done and we fade away into dust, the constant that remains is love. Love binds you together and blinds you at times. Love heals your pain and fills your hearts. Love makes good on all things and makes all things good. You've been told throughout the ages that love is the answer. This is because you came from love and will return to love. Love is eternal, brave and true. Live your life with love for others. Live your life with love for yourself. And live your life with love at its centre and watch how the world will respond with love to you."

Another polite ripple of applause broke out amongst the crowd. But where there had been shouting and cheering for other speakers, the crowd offered up a sense of reverence to the words the young man was speaking.

"And so, I come to the last step towards real success. Some may suggest this isn't truly a step you need to take, but more of a lesson or understanding. The final step is to accept you live in a paradoxical world. Much of what you believe is good for you often turns out to be unhelpful. Sometimes, our toughest times teach us our greatest lessons. Stop trying to live a life without pain, grief or sorrow. It's simply not possible nor why you are here. Stop expecting to live a life of pure joy, achievement and success. You cannot feel the deepest love without experiencing the deepest pain. Often our greatest sense of love and healing appears during the most painful times in our lives. If you've failed in business, you've found out more about your strengths and your character than if the business hadn't failed. If you've been in a failed relationship, you will have discovered what makes you happy, and unhappy, and perhaps put new boundaries into future relationships. If an idea has failed, you may have uncovered new ideas you hadn't previously considered. And if you've lost someone you love, you've touched the deepest love of all. You see, the world you inhabit is designed to be a paradox. Sometimes, what you think is impossible leads you to discover what is possible. Sometimes, the unexpected, or that which seems out of place, is there deliberately to move us, focus us or simply bring our attention back to what is right about our world. So, ladies and gentlemen, if you follow these ten steps, you will find life runs more smoothly, peace comes to you more naturally and real success is yours. My steps for real success are your steps towards a life that will Be the Best it can be. Thank you!"

There was a momentary pause as John stepped back from the lectern. The audience appeared unsure how to respond and even whether applause was appropriate. Then a ripple began, followed by more applause, followed by cheering and then roars of approval as people got to their feet. People were putting down their notepads and clambering onto their seats to applaud. Some people rushed down towards the stage, waving their programmes, wanting John to sign them. Security staff appeared and tried to stop too many people reaching the stage and causing a crush.

From their seats high up in the arena, David and Lucy applauded and cheered. David, with tears of pride rolling down his cheeks at the young man's speech, was overcome with admiration. He knew much of what John had said; David had heard many of these words from Michael and from some of the other people he'd met over the past few weeks. But his words rang true for David, and like the rest of the crowd, he got up onto his seat and cheered.

John moved to the edge of the stage and leant down to sign his name, but too many people were reaching out to touch him and the security guards were beginning to pull them back. John was kneeling now at the front of the stage and David wondered whether his smart pinstripe suit would survive.

And then he saw them.

David looked up at the big screens to check if what he could see was real.

In between John's shoes and his suit trousers were scarlet socks.

And David realised where he'd seen them before.

23.

The crowd applauded John for more than ten minutes, during which he signed autographs and slowly made his way to the side of the stage and with a final wave, he disappeared.

David had been sitting down for the last five minutes of John's applause. His knees had given way and he felt light-headed. Lucy, in a panic, thought he was having another heart attack and asked Becky to get some help. David had pulled Becky back and reassured her and Lucy that he was fine.

Once John had left the stage, the crowd started to move back into the outer concourse for another break. The buzz of excitement at the ten rules for life which John had outlined was still evident in the bars and coffee shops. People were asking about John and where he'd come from. No one seemed to know anything about him.

Except for David.

"He was amazing wasn't he?" said Lucy as they walked down the stairs towards a well-needed coffee break. "Did you say he was that young lad who works for one of your suppliers? Didn't you know he was a speaker and a good one too? Have you heard him speak this way before?"

"Gosh Lucy, that's a stack of questions. Right now, I'm still flabbergasted by what he said rather than who he is. His words were spoken with such authority. It was spooky."

"I know, the whole arena fell silent and seemed to hang on his every word, didn't they? I wish Annabel had been here. She'd have loved him."

"I think everyone loved him. It was hard not to."

They arrived in one of the long queues for coffee and waited patiently. David was lost in his own thoughts. Who was John Benjamin? Who was Michael? Why are they wearing scarlet socks? And who were all the other people he'd met over the past few weeks?

Once they'd made small talk with others in the queue, who were all equally blown away by John's talk, they made their way back in for what was billed as the main attraction. Unfortunately, it turned out to be nothing more than a sales pitch for Robin Anton's courses and programmes. The atmosphere felt quite flat following the amazing reaction to Andy and John. It became clear from the crowd's reaction that the audience saw through this global speaker. While certainly of good intent, he all too obviously had a marketing machine behind him which was primarily aimed at convincing people to attend his courses.

David recalled why he'd been cynical about these sorts of events before, and Mr Anton completely vindicated his earlier stance. The atmosphere was very muted during his talk, as if the main event had already happened. In most people's minds, it already had. Even Lucy was muted about her appreciation once he'd finished speaking and people began to file out of the arena.

"That was a bit of an anti-climax wasn't it?" she said as they stood up from their seats.

David smiled. "That's because he was seriously upstaged by John and Andy. Their messages were far stronger than the same old story of setting big goals and having big dreams. We've heard all that sort of stuff before. As John clearly showed, and Andy too, there's much more to real success than just positive thinking."

They strolled back together to the hotel to pack their bags and collect their things. Lucy had organised for a 1pm checkout so they were able to pack and be downstairs settling their bill by just after 1pm. They chatted little while they were packing, and David felt a little punch-drunk from what he had witnessed. He felt that his whole life had been laid out in front of him. Meeting Andy again, followed by John's ten steps for real success, had given him a new perspective. But it was also a perspective which felt familiar in some way. David felt he knew some of the messages John had delivered and he was now puzzled as to who this man with scarlet socks really was.

As they got into a taxi, Lucy broke the silence. "I remember, John Benjamin came up to us and said hello, didn't he? But he never mentioned he was speaking, did he?"

"No, he didn't love."

"But the man who spoke on that stage felt much older than the young man we met. He spoke with such authority and clarity; I could've listened to him for hours. He had such presence as well. Not something you would associate with a young man. He wasn't even dressed like a young man either. His suit was quite old fashioned and yet he was captivating. I felt almost hypnotised by him."

"I think there were many in the crowd who felt the same way Lucy. More importantly his simple messages were easy to understand and made total sense. I've heard some of them before, but there was a freshness to them that gave them more resonance. For me, he was the highlight of the whole conference. I can't wait to see him again when he next comes into the office."

The taxi journey was short and brought them back to Birmingham International station where, after a short wait, they were able to board the next train back to Euston. After David had placed their bags in the luggage area, he joined Lucy who'd already found a couple of empty seats.

"I feel drained but uplifted," she said.

"Me too. But I'm glad we came. After the last few weeks, I know, now more than ever, that I need to live my life in a more balanced way. I'm going to start by forgiving myself for the mess I got us into. I'm sorry Lucy, I really am."

"But we've talked about this already. I'm just glad I've still got you. Remember what John said about paradoxes. Yes, we've had some difficult times recently, but it's just made us appreciate what we've got now hasn't it? Maybe we'd never have attended this conference if those things hadn't happened."

"I guess so, but it's sad it takes a business crisis, a heart attack and a chance meeting with an old man called Michael in the park to get me back on track."

"An old man in a park? Who are you talking about?"

"Never mind honey. It's just I met an old man in the park on my morning walk a month or so ago and I'm beginning to wonder if he was John's father. He said a few things to me that John also expressed in his talk. But John said to me that he'd met this chap called Michael too. I don't know really, but all I do know is that John's message must be heard by more people. He's working for a plumbing materials business when he's clearly got a much higher calling."

"But John said our calling needn't be anything grand. He might be passionate about helping people in business and he's certainly good at it. Look how he helped you. Who are we to judge where his values lie? His current role might be helping him live his life with purpose."

"Yes, it's easy to judge people isn't it until we know their story. There was much more to Andy Smith, sorry, Drew Jones, that I didn't know. There's much about John I don't know too but we all jump to conclusions based on our own lives I guess."

"I think we've just followed about four or five of the steps for real success in this conversation! One thing that did puzzle me in John's speech was when he talked about listening to the silence. How can you listen to nothing if your mind is already full of daily worries and concerns?"

David smiled.

"Finding the silence isn't easy in our busy lives. I remember when I met Samuel in the church in the park, the noise of London disappeared, and I could sense a connection with something much greater than me. You know I turned away from religion a long time ago Lucy, but on the day of the conference, and hearing what happened to Samuel since, I do wonder whether John means we must make time and find the spaces where we can be quiet, to connect to something higher and more intelligent than us. When we can clear our minds of our busy thoughts, we can then find solutions which have been evading us for ages."

"I've got lots of friends who meditate, and they say it really helps them", said Lucy. "But I guess prayers in church would be the same or taking a walk through the woods or finding anywhere where you can switch off your phone, leave behind the worries of the day and listen to your intuition. That's what John said didn't he?"

They talked more about John's talk and then their flow of conversation was interrupted by the ticket inspector. After David had handed him the tickets, he noticed he was writing something on the back of his ticket. He handed the ticket back to David and walked down the train, not checking anyone else's tickets, which seemed odd.

David turned over his ticket and on the back was the same quote he'd read on the red envelope in his hotel room the previous day.

'Faith shows the reality of what we hope for; it is the evidence of things we cannot see. Hebrews 11.1'

"What's that David?"

"Just my ticket love."

"But there's something written on it. Let me see." Lucy snatched the ticket from David's hand.

"Why would a ticket inspector write something like that on your ticket? That's proper weird. A religious nutcase loose on the train. That's all we need."

David took the ticket from Lucy and for the rest of the journey they mostly sat in silence with their own thoughts. Lucy was checking social media on her phone and David even slept for part of the journey. He was woken by the train guard announcing they were heading into Euston station. They gathered their bags, got off the train and headed for the exit and the taxi rank where they were soon picked up and were heading for home.

As the taxi made its way towards Highgate, David could hear the radio. As it was approaching 4pm, the hourly news bulletin was being announced. David listened through the glass between the driver and himself and Lucy.

The announcer started the news.

"Today's headlines at 4pm. The prime minister has welcomed the American ambassador today for talks about the crisis in Europe over trade."

David began to switch off, realising the news would be the usual brand of depressing and negative headlines. After a few minutes, Lucy sat bolt upright. "Turn it up," she shouted to the driver.

The driver duly obliged by turning up the volume on the radio.

"Unconfirmed reports are coming in that a man has been killed in Birmingham after falling in front of a speeding train at Birmingham International station. Eyewitnesses report seeing a child running towards the edge of the platform as the train approached and a young man in a pinstripe suit attempting to stop the child and in doing so sacrificing his own life. There were many people on the platform, as a large convention had just concluded nearby. The police are confident they will be able to quickly identify the man who was killed, as some are suggesting it could be one of the speakers at the conference. More details as we get them."

"Oh my God David. That sounds like John Benjamin doesn't it? They said it was a young man in a pinstripe suit. Surely it can't be. Oh God no, I so hope it isn't."

David took Lucy's hand. "I'm sure it isn't love, but whoever it was, it's a horrible way to go. Particularly if he was trying to save a child from falling in front of the train too. Gosh, what a horrible thing to witness for all the people at the station."

The taxi pulled up outside their house and the front door opened. Annabel came running down the drive to meet them, throwing her arms around Lucy.

"Welcome back Mum and of course, you too Dad."

"We've only been gone a couple of days, you big softie," said David.

"Have you heard the news?" said Annabel. "A young man has been killed at the same train station as you were leaving today. I think it happened just after your train had left. When I heard it on the news, my heart skipped a beat. They said he was a speaker at your conference though - someone called John Benjamin?"

David stopped as they got to the house.

"No, please God no. Not John. Oh no... John was such a fine young man, with his whole life ahead of him. And what he said was so powerful and important. This is devastating."

They walked into the house and put down their bags.

"I'll put the kettle on," said Annabel. "Let's have a cup of tea, to help us all recover from this awful shock."

Lucy started to get some cups from the cupboard while Annabel placed some tea bags into the teapot.

"Gosh, this is so awful," said Lucy. "He was so young. He was just beginning to get into his stride too. You should've heard his talk Annabel. You'd have loved it. I guess that talk and his ten steps for real success will now be his legacy. Do we know how old he was? Did they say on the news?"

"Thirty-three apparently, according to the BBC," said Annabel. "The weird thing is some people are reporting having seen a figure in a black hoodie pushing a child towards the edge of the platform. The police say there's no trace of the character dressed in black and eyewitnesses say he just disappeared into the shadows. They can't even find any trace of the hooded man on the CCTV footage either. Sounds really creepy doesn't it?"

"Did they say anything about the child or the train driver?" said Lucy. "The parents must have been terribly shaken up and the poor driver of the train – how horrible for them."

"Yes Mum, the reporter said that the train driver reported being blinded by a bright light just before he hit the man who fell in front of his train. The little boy is completely unharmed, and his parents have been taken to hospital suffering from shock. It's all so sad isn't it?"

Annabel poured the boiling water into the teapot and stirred the tea bags and water together. Lucy added the milk to the cups, and they all sat down around the kitchen table.

"Let's try and talk about something else. Come on then, how was the conference?"

"It was incredible Annabel, even your dad enjoyed it. Gosh David, what's the matter?"

David was crying. "I feel we've just lost someone very important. And it sounds like he sacrificed his own life to save another. I'm trying to see where the paradox will be in the pain his family will feel and the emptiness I can already feel. It's not like I knew him well, but it's as if I've lost a part of me. I just feel incredibly sad. I can't even talk about the conference to be honest. That doesn't seem important now."

David put his head in his hands and quietly sobbed. Lucy rubbed his back to comfort him, but Annabel looked perplexed. "I'm sorry Dad, it's a horrible thing that's happened. Hopefully, they will find out who pushed the child towards the edge of the platform."

"I think, in a way, perhaps we all did," said David.

Lucy shook her head at Annabel, who was now looking even more confused.

"Why don't you go and take a shower David, and we can unpack later. It's been a long and emotional day."

"I think I will love. Thank you."

David left the kitchen and headed upstairs. He went into the bathroom, removed his clothes and got into the shower, allowing the hot water to gently ease some of the tensions. As his mind cleared, he asked the silence a single question. Why?

"It was for you," came the reply.

David didn't understand the response from the silence. He got out of the shower and went into the bedroom to put on some fresh clothes.

Going to the chest of drawers in the bedroom, he opened the top drawer and took out some clean boxer shorts and put them on. Then he opened the next drawer to grab some socks.

He stopped.

Lying on top of all his other socks was a pair of scarlet socks, tied together with a white ribbon. Attached to the socks with the ribbon was a rolled-up piece of paper. David lifted the red socks from the drawer and sat down on the bed. His hands were shaking as he placed the socks gently on the bed. He untied the ribbon and unrolled the small piece of paper.

Some words had been written by hand:

Ten Steps for Real Success:

1. **Find the silence.** It is here you will find the greatest answers to your deepest questions.

2. **Trust in synchronicity.** There are no such things as chance or coincidence. Be open to the impossible and watch the possible emerge in your life.

3. **Seek your purpose first.** Discover your passions, understand your values, recognise your talents and hear your calling. Set your compass by your purpose and your goals in life will be congruent with who you are.

4. **Aim for less.** Find joy in the small things. Remember that as our years progress, we realise more and more how little we need to be happy.

5. **Recognise when it's your move.** Your life is in harmony with all there is so if you're stuck, it might be your turn to act. Listen to the silence, then make a move.

6. **Look out for the weeds.** Notice your thoughts and watch out for the blockages. Nothing can stop the forces of good so keep moving forwards, even when fear takes hold.

7. **Don't judge others until you know their story.** None of us are without faults, shame or errors. If we judge others for their story, we too will be judged for ours.

8. **Forgiveness is the gateway to progress.** We must forgive others and ourselves and when we do, we move forwards with wisdom.

9. **Love is all there is.** You came from love and will return to love. Live your life with love for others and for yourself.

10. **Life is a paradox.** When you seek joy, you will often find pain. When you experience loss, you will often discover love in its purest form. You see things out of place which are divinely placed. You notice imperfections when everything is perfect.

BE THE
BEST.
CONFERENCE

David, let these scarlet socks be a reminder you should always look for the good in everything and accept what can often appear as uncomfortable may just be your gateway to future success, happiness and contentment.

Your friend,
The Man with Scarlet Socks.

'Faith shows the reality of what we hope
for; it is the evidence of things we cannot see.'
Hebrews 11

David held the piece of paper in his hand, knowing he'd been given a blueprint for the rest of his life and the real success he'd been searching for. He knew too that the people he'd met during the most uncomfortable phase of his life were all signposting him to a much better future. It had indeed been a beautiful paradox. He knew that the man with scarlet socks was someone magical who had sacrificed his own life to save another.

He turned over the piece of paper on which the rules had been written and in the top right-hand corner was the logo of the Be the Best conference. And in the centre of the paper was the quote from the red envelope in the hotel and on the train ticket on his journey home.

'Faith shows the reality of what we hope for; it is the evidence of things we cannot see. Hebrews 11.1'

David stared at the paper from the conference, the ten steps for real success and the scarlet socks in his hands. He'd no idea how the socks or the note could have been placed amongst his own clothes and how the ten steps for real success could have been written and sent to him before he'd even got home.

He held the scarlet socks in his hands and thought about Michael and John. Tears welled up as he realised that the child saved by the man with scarlet socks wasn't the only soul on the platform on a busy train station in Birmingham. He realised the man with the scarlet socks had saved him too along with every other person who ever came into contact with that magical man.

And for the first time, he truly understood.

THE END

Acknowledgements

This story was written four times. Each time, it took a different direction until it finally landed as you've read it here. There are many people who directly or indirectly contributed to the creation of The Man with Scarlet Socks, from friends who've journeyed with me through the phases of my life to people I've met by chance, that shaped some of the characters in the book.

I'd like to acknowledge the input of Mark Beaumont-Thomas, my editor who reshaped my manuscript, and Sam Pearce from SWATT Books who helped bring the book into its first publication.

Most of all, I will be forever grateful for the support of my family as I journeyed directly through phases of David's story. Thank you for allowing me to continue to dream and find my faith, despite the hardship it brought to you all at times.

About the Author

Paul Harris is a speaker, writer, facilitator and author who is recognised as a thought leader in people development and authentic, personal success. His business, Real Success, is a UK-based training, coaching and consultancy organisation that helps companies to build a cohesive culture through a holistic approach to staff management and development. Paul's expertise in his field draws on over 30 years' business experience. See more at www.real-success.co.uk.

Paul has developed a unique personality profiling tool called VITA Profiling; for more information, visit www.vitaprofiling.com

Paul is available for presentations, keynote speaking and workshop facilitation. He can be contacted through the UK Real Success office on +44 121 296 6669.

Paul is married to Samantha and has three children. He travels all over the UK and Europe to work with and inspire his clients.

The Man with Scarlet Socks is his first novel.

Printed in Great Britain
by Amazon